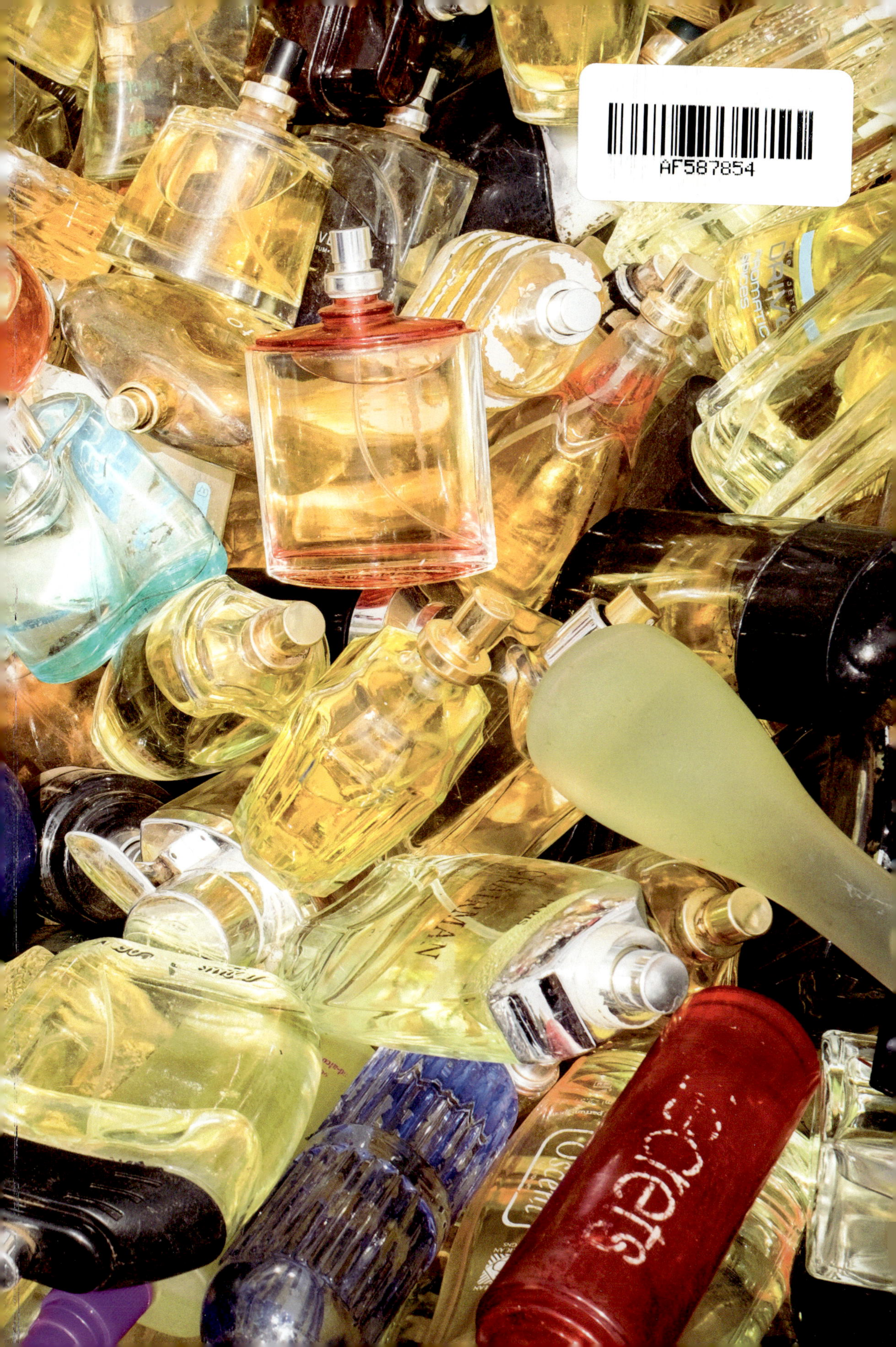

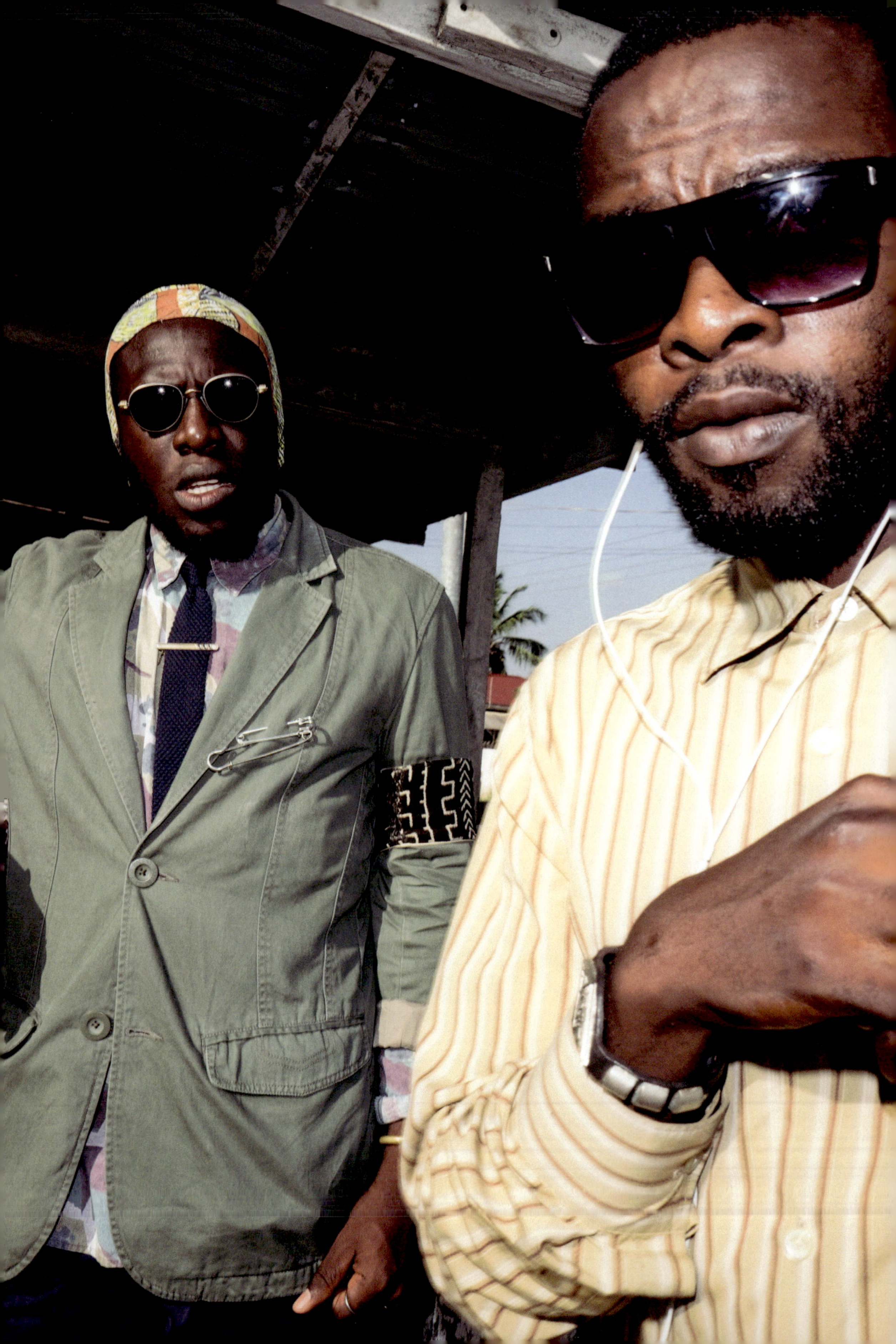

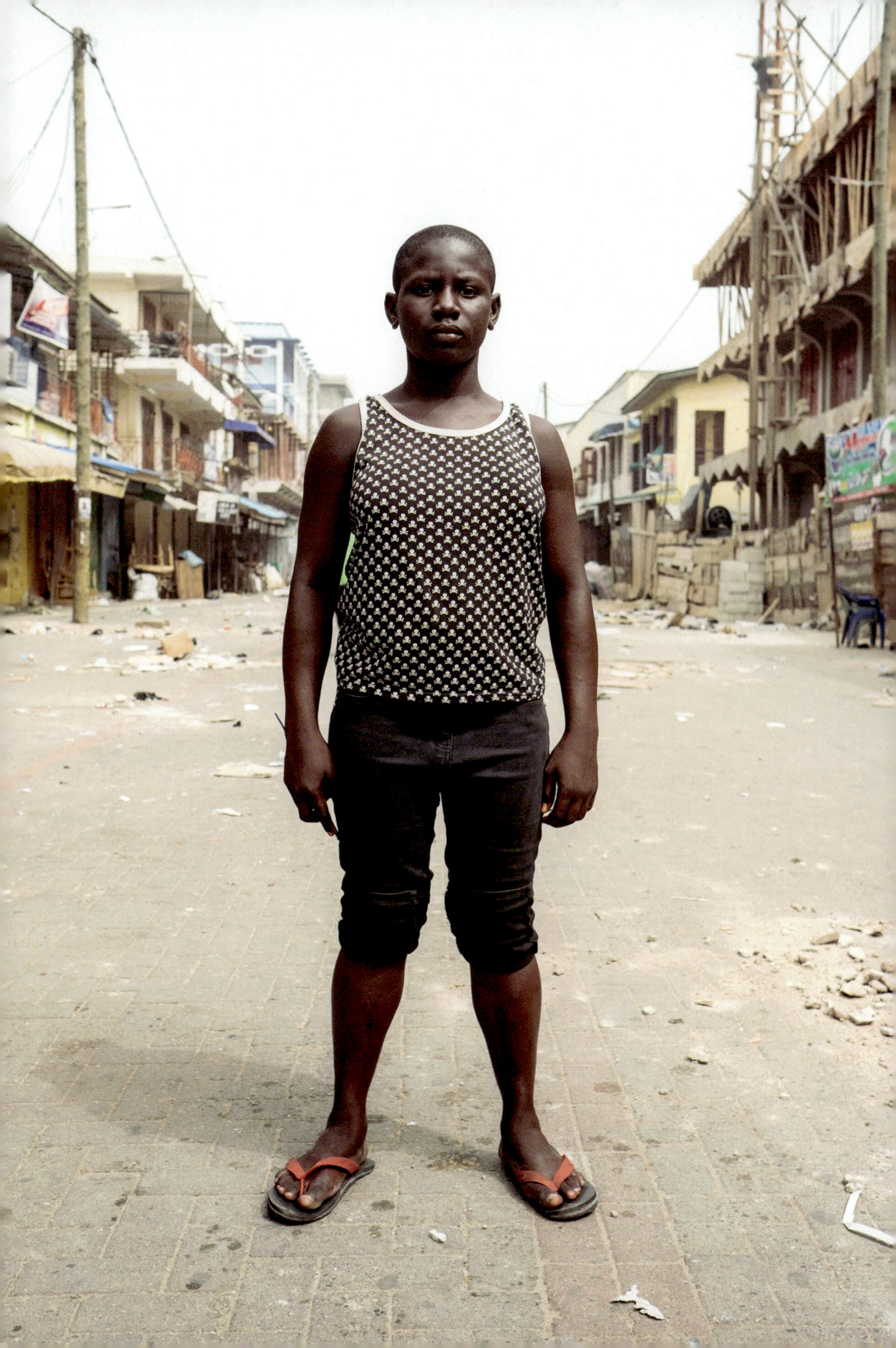

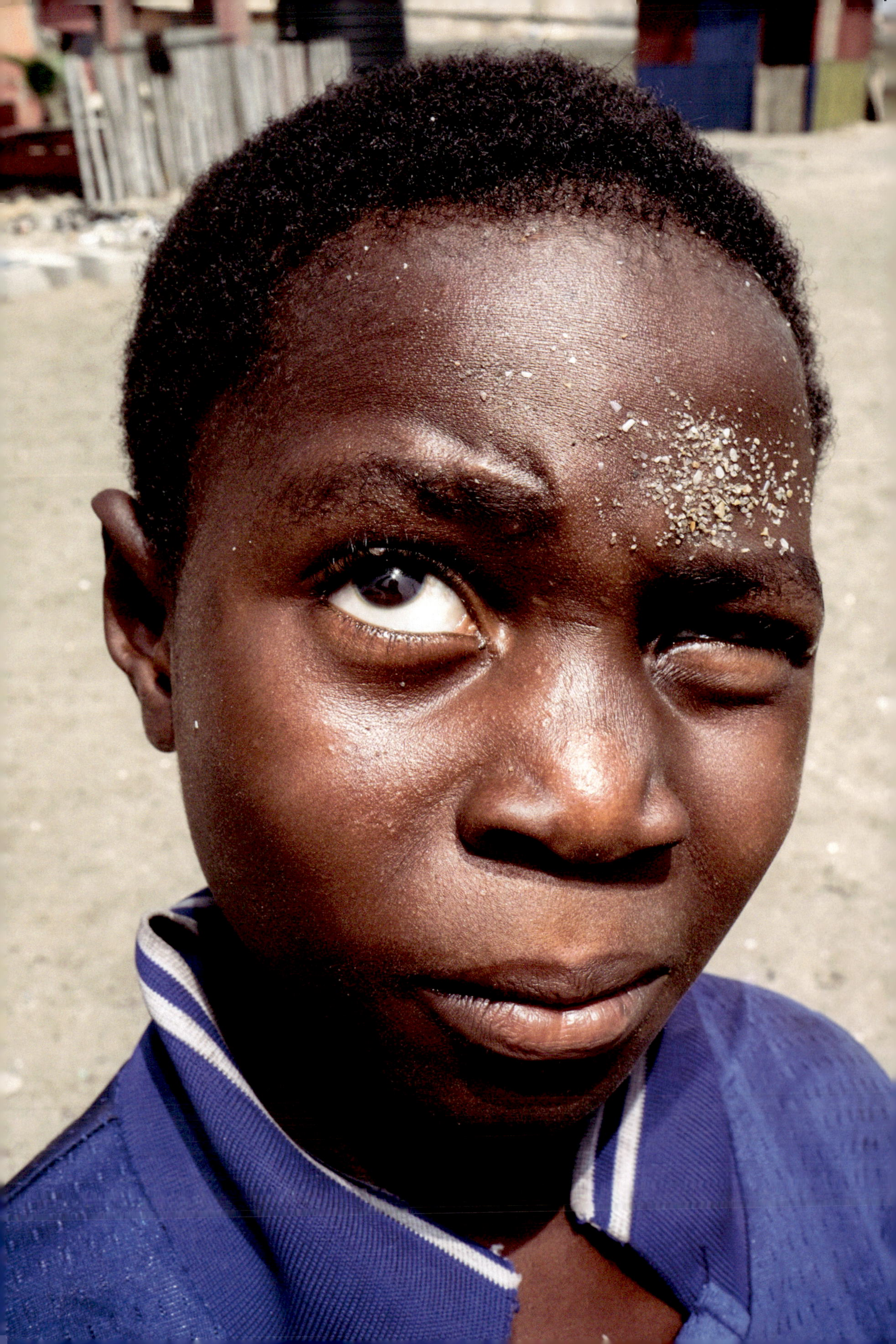

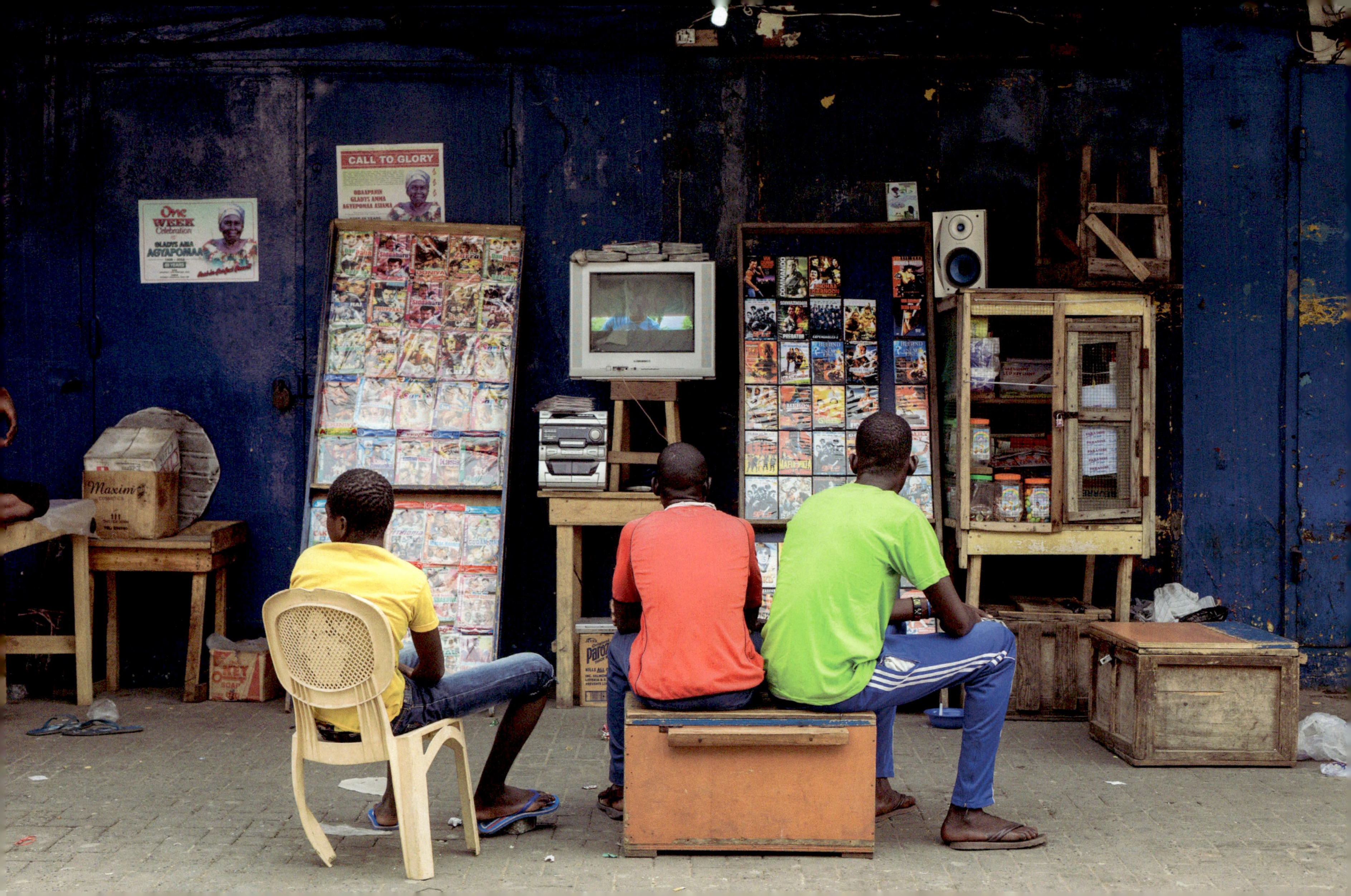

One WEEK Celebration
AGYAPOMAA
CALL TO GLORY
COMMANDO
Maxim

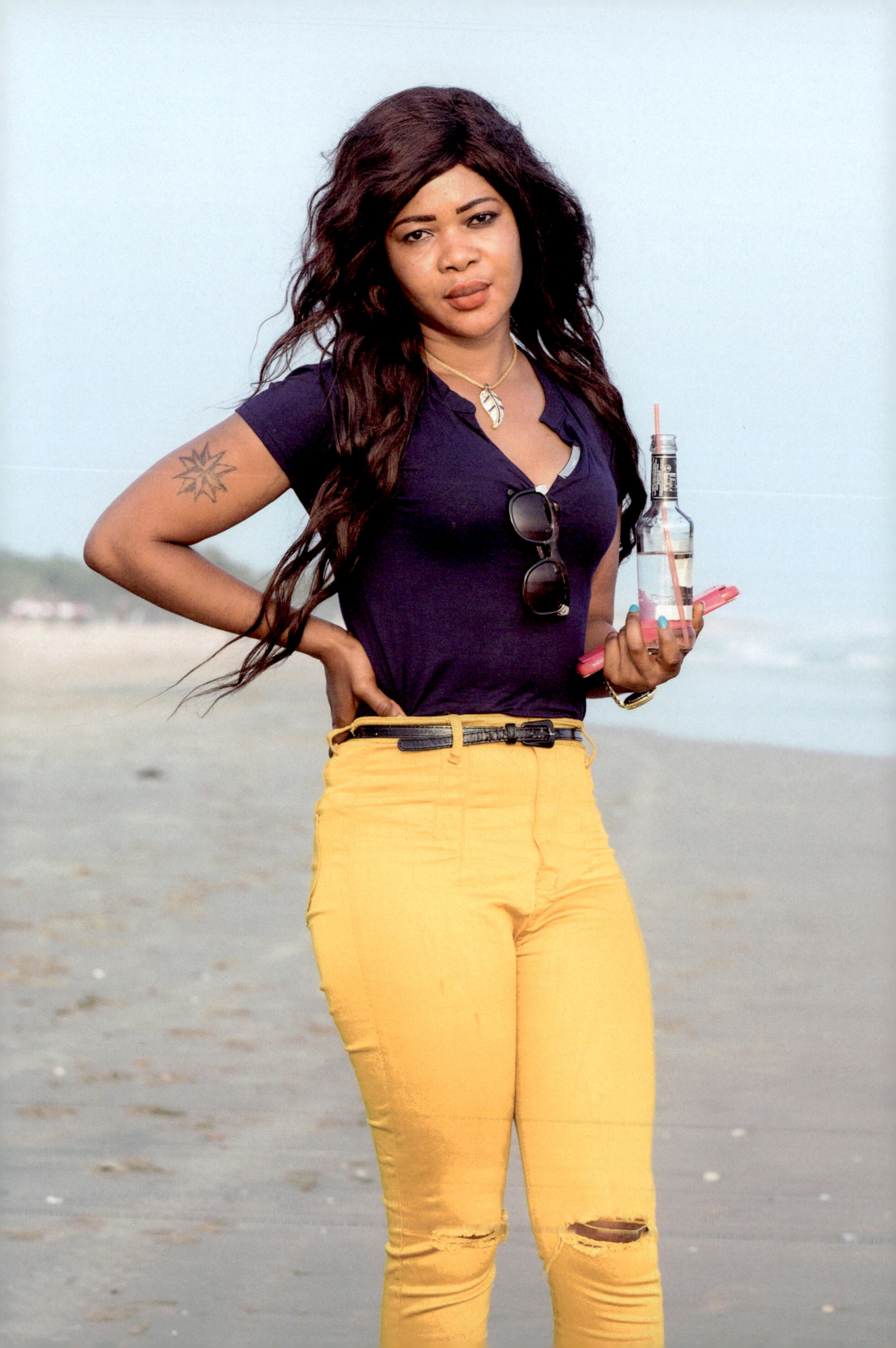

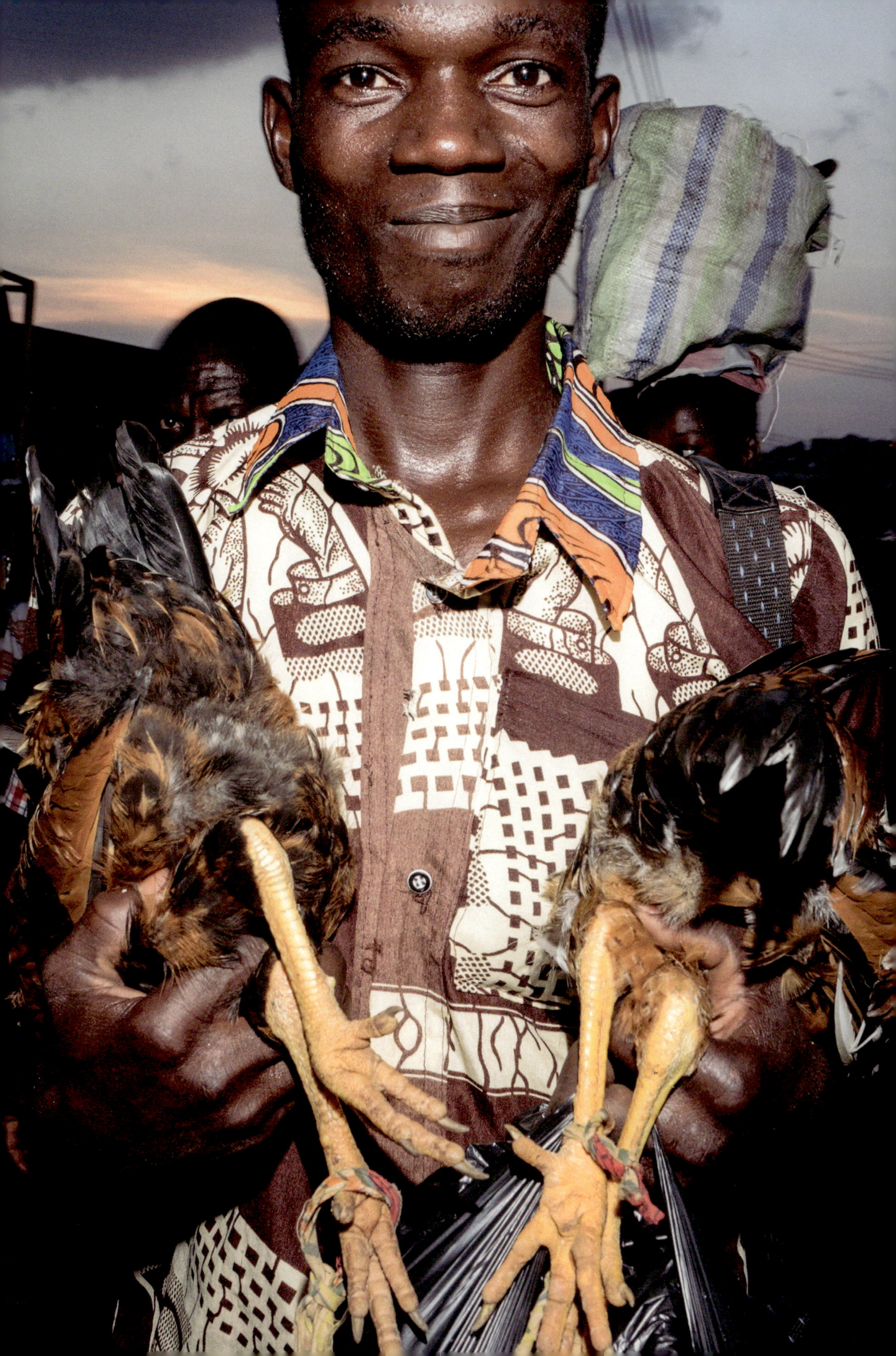

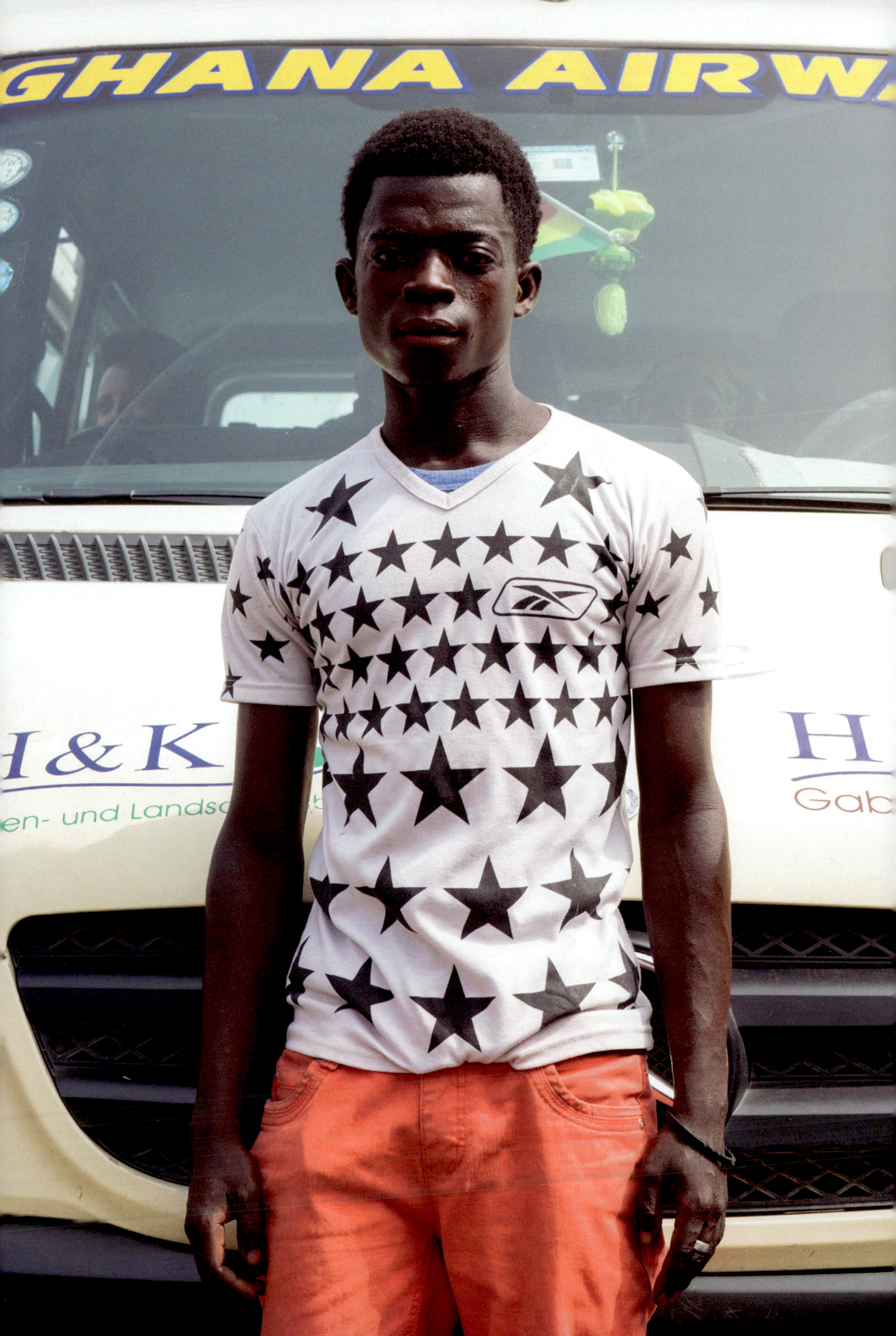
GHANA AIRW
H&K
en- und Landsc
H
Gab

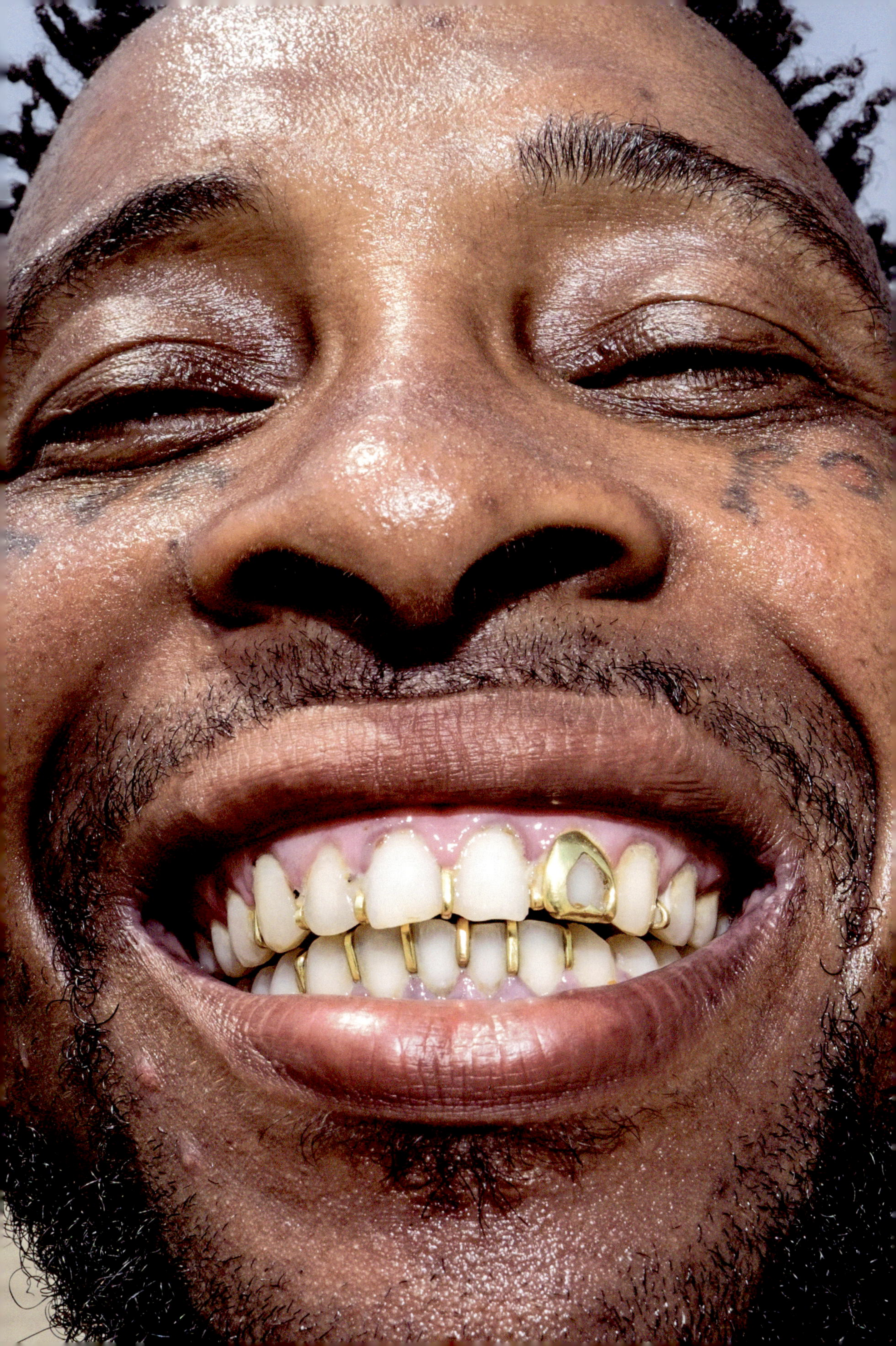

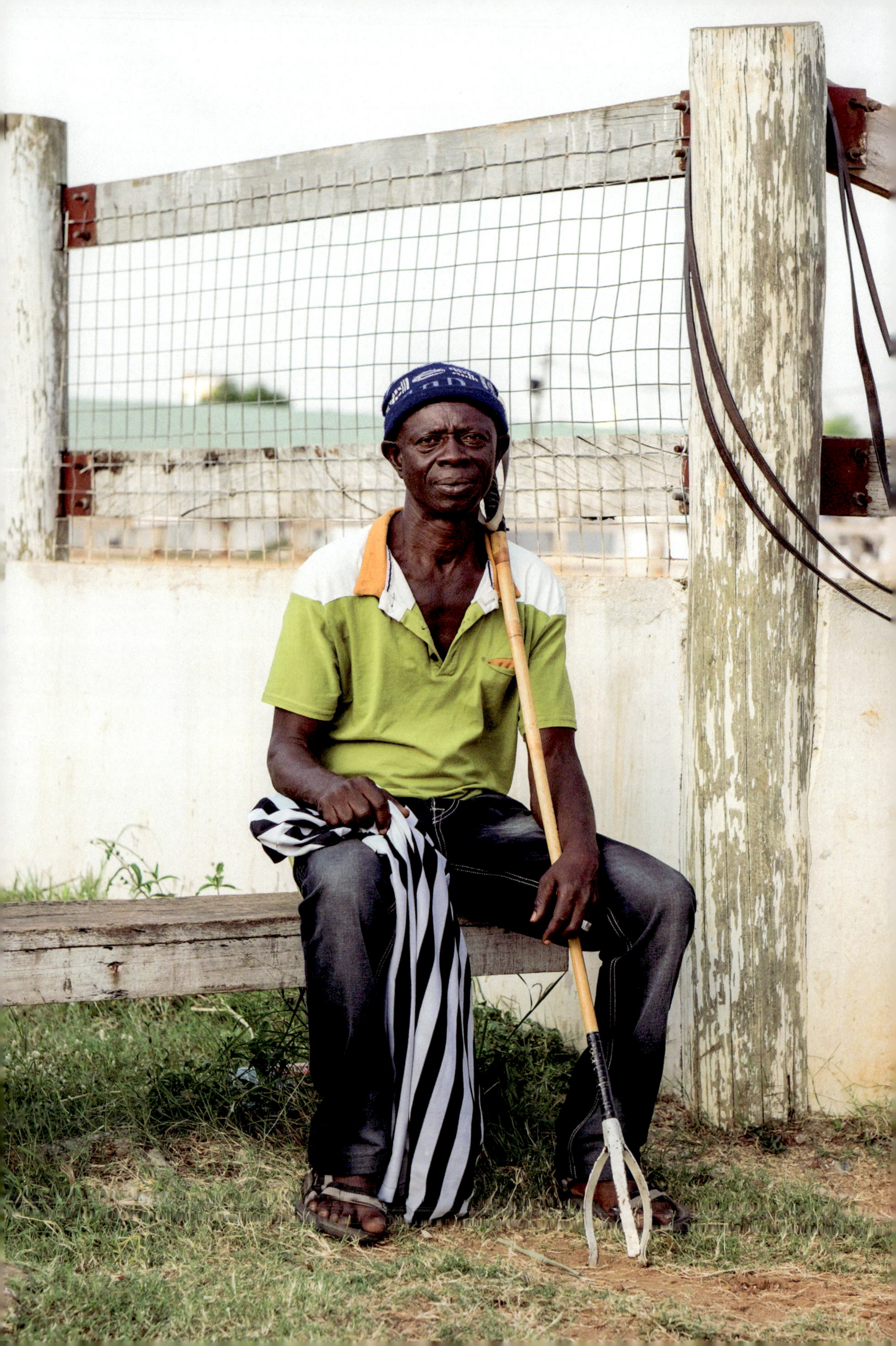

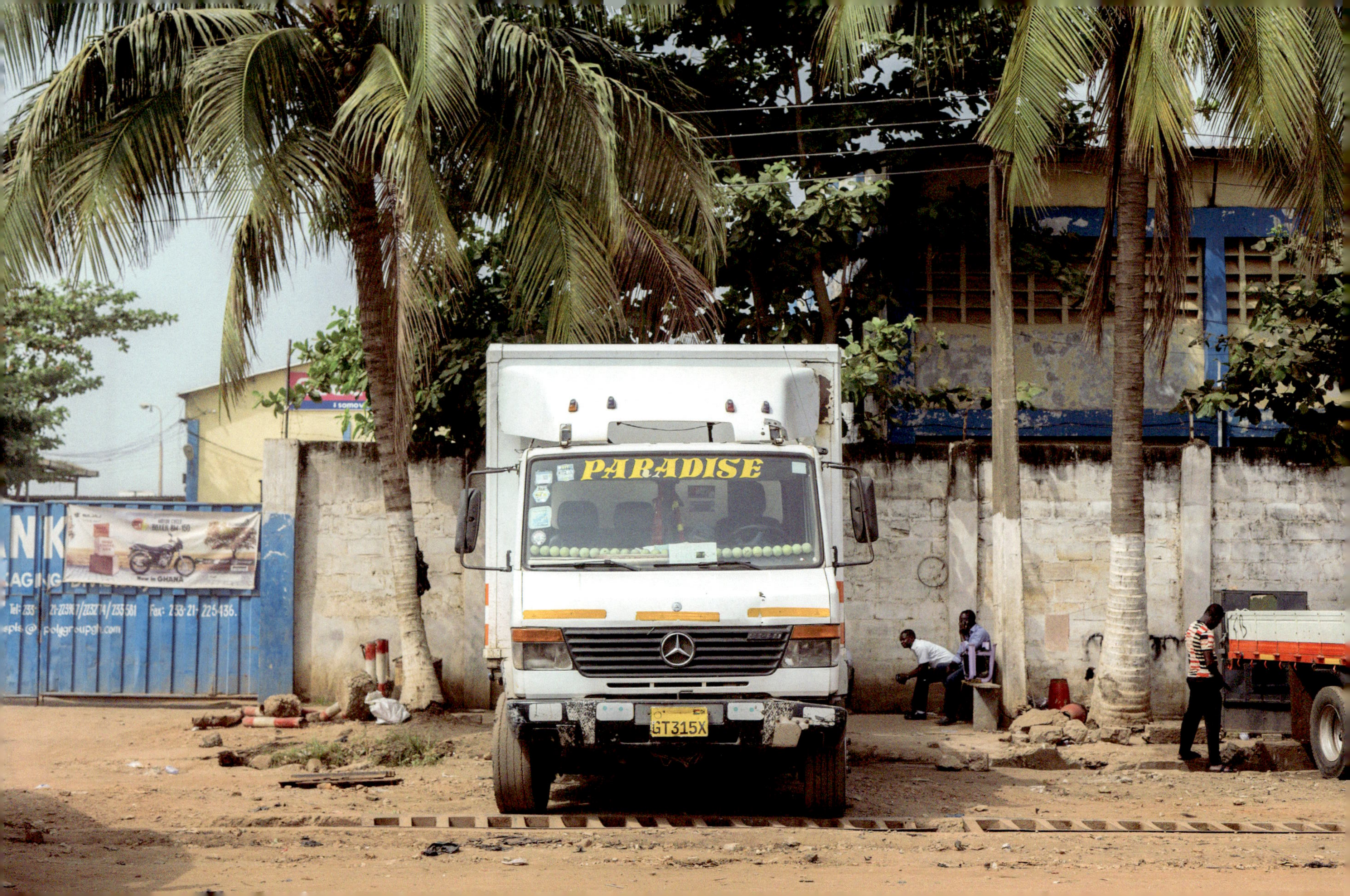
PARADISE
GT315X

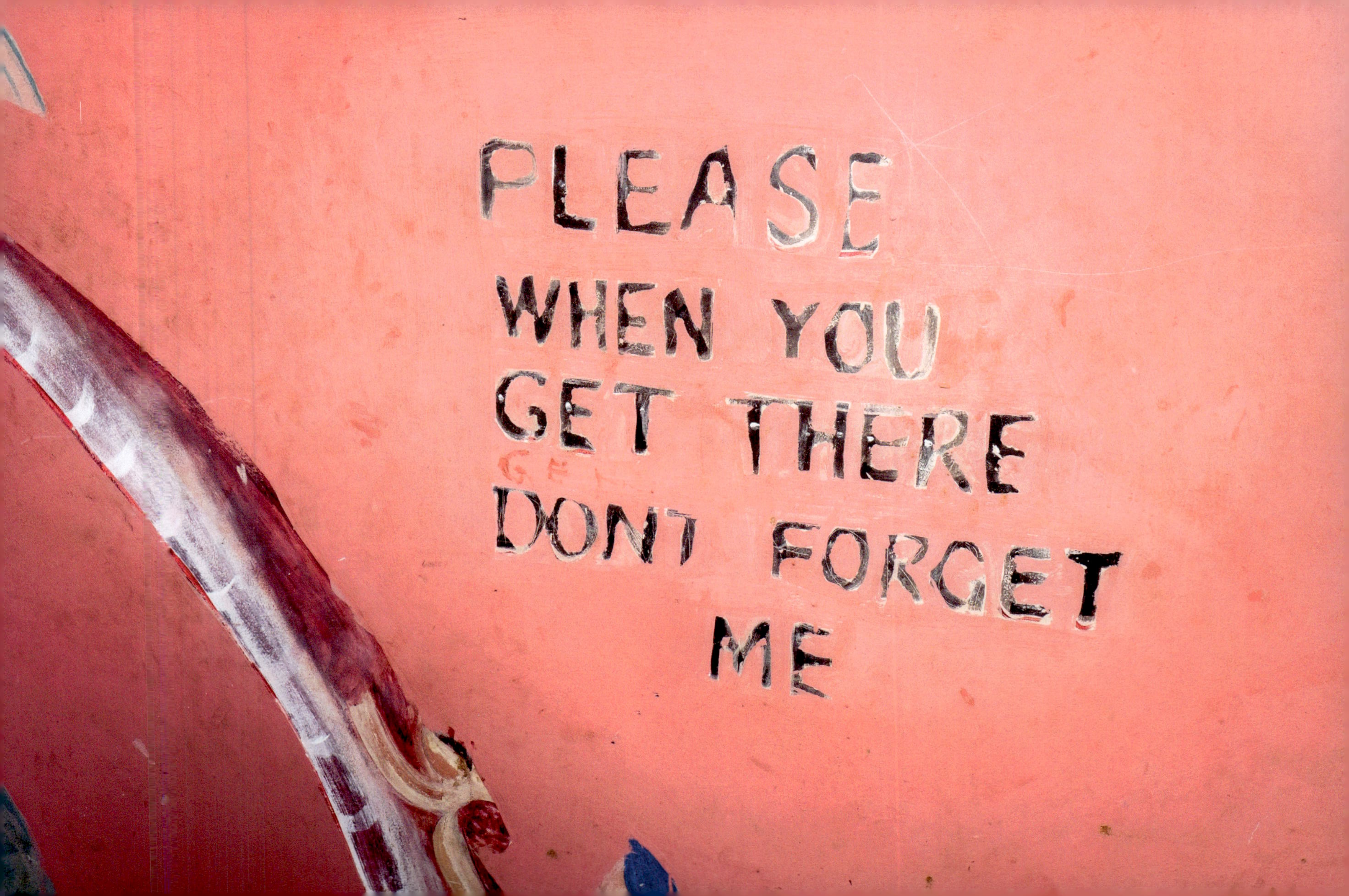

PLEASE
WHEN YOU
GET THERE
DONT FORGET
ME

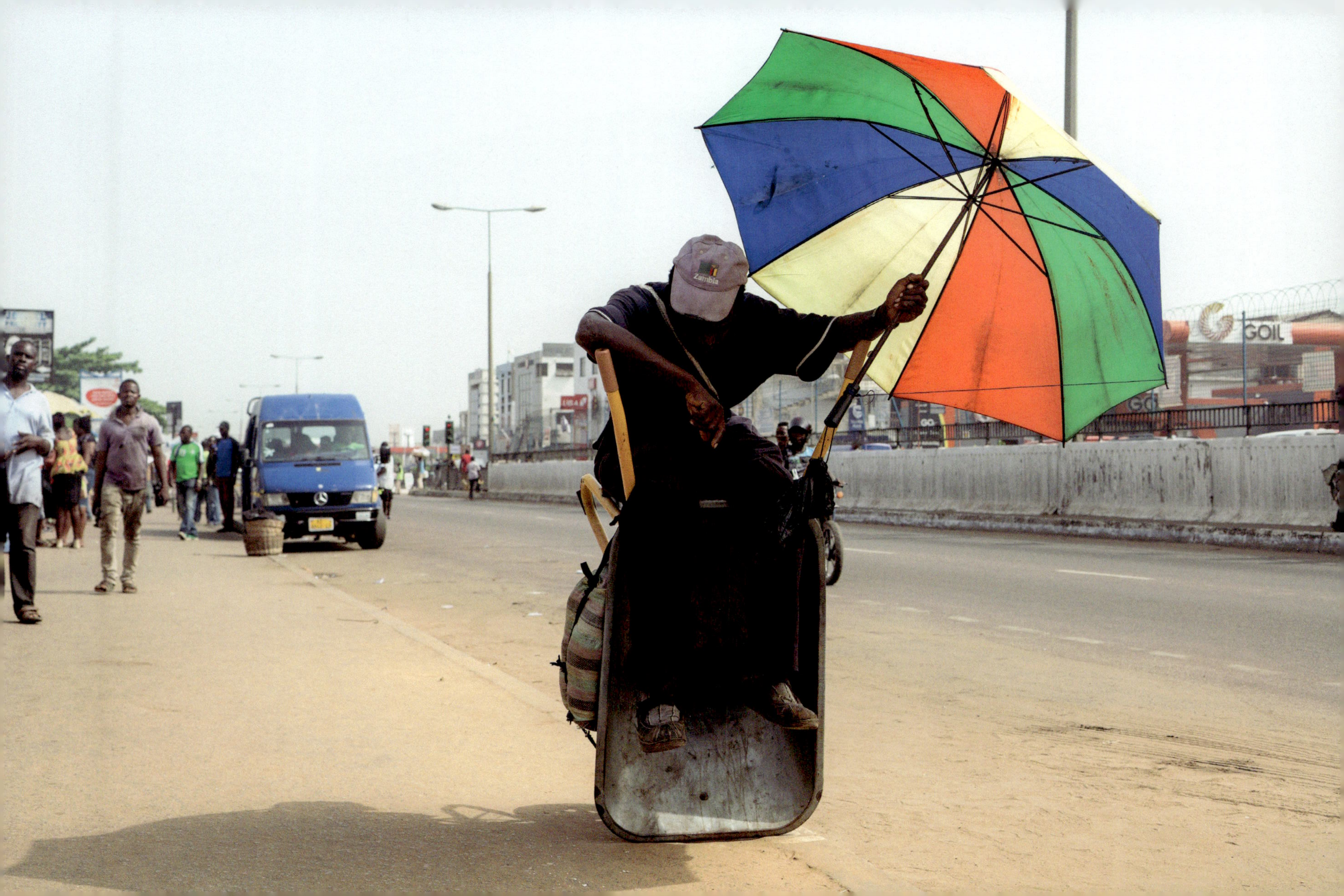
GOIL
Zambia

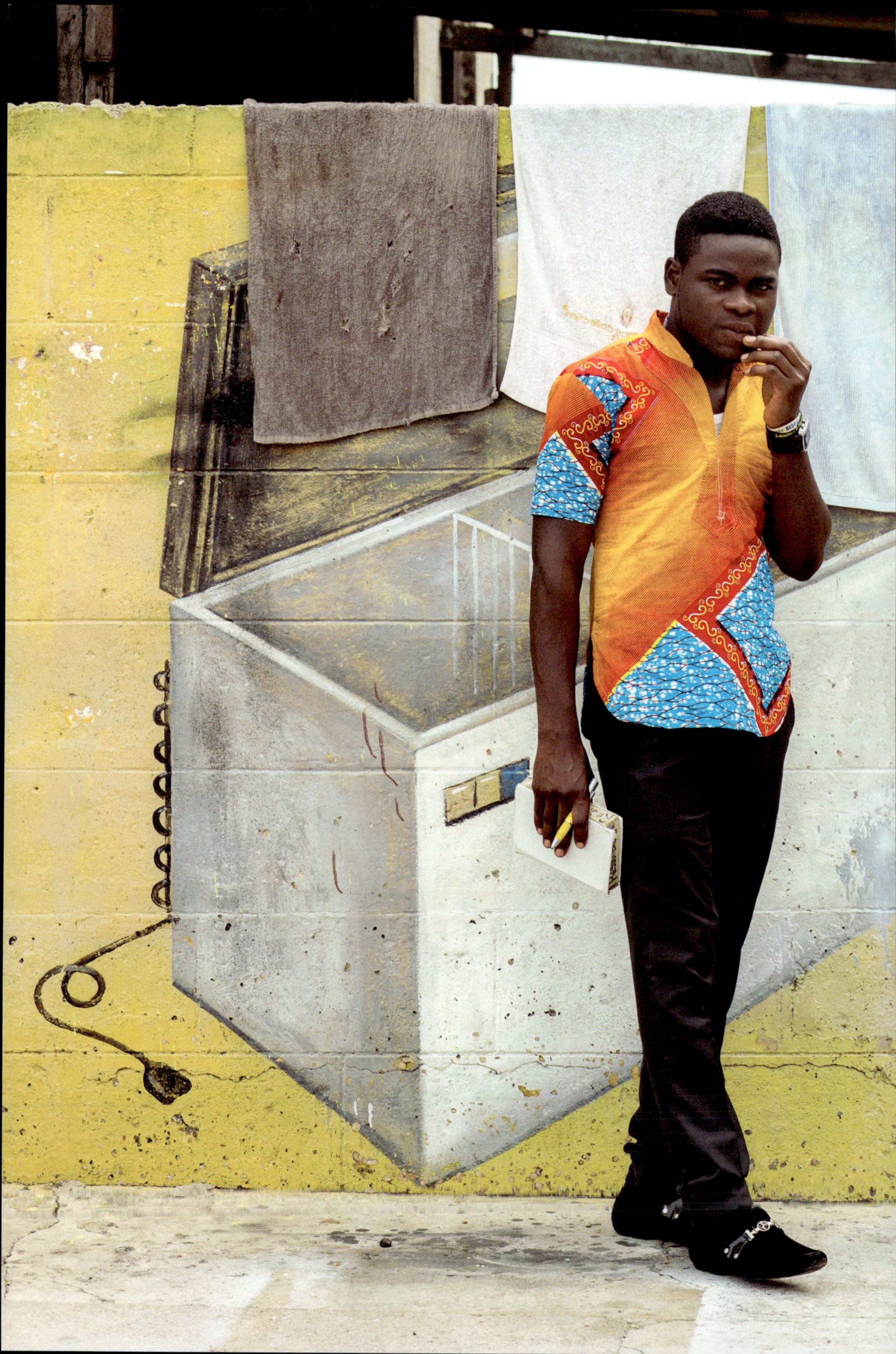

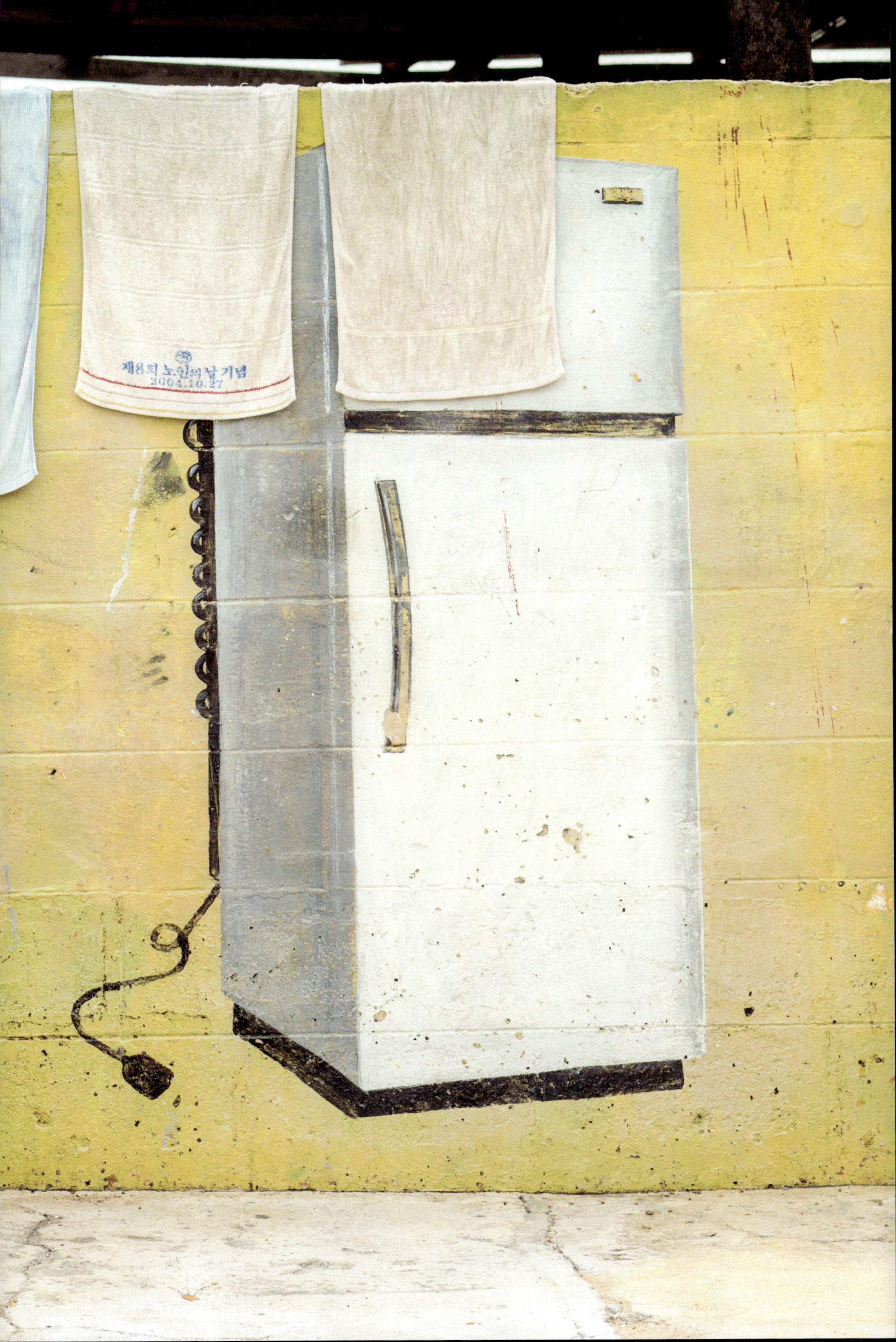
제8회 노인의날 기념
2004.10.27

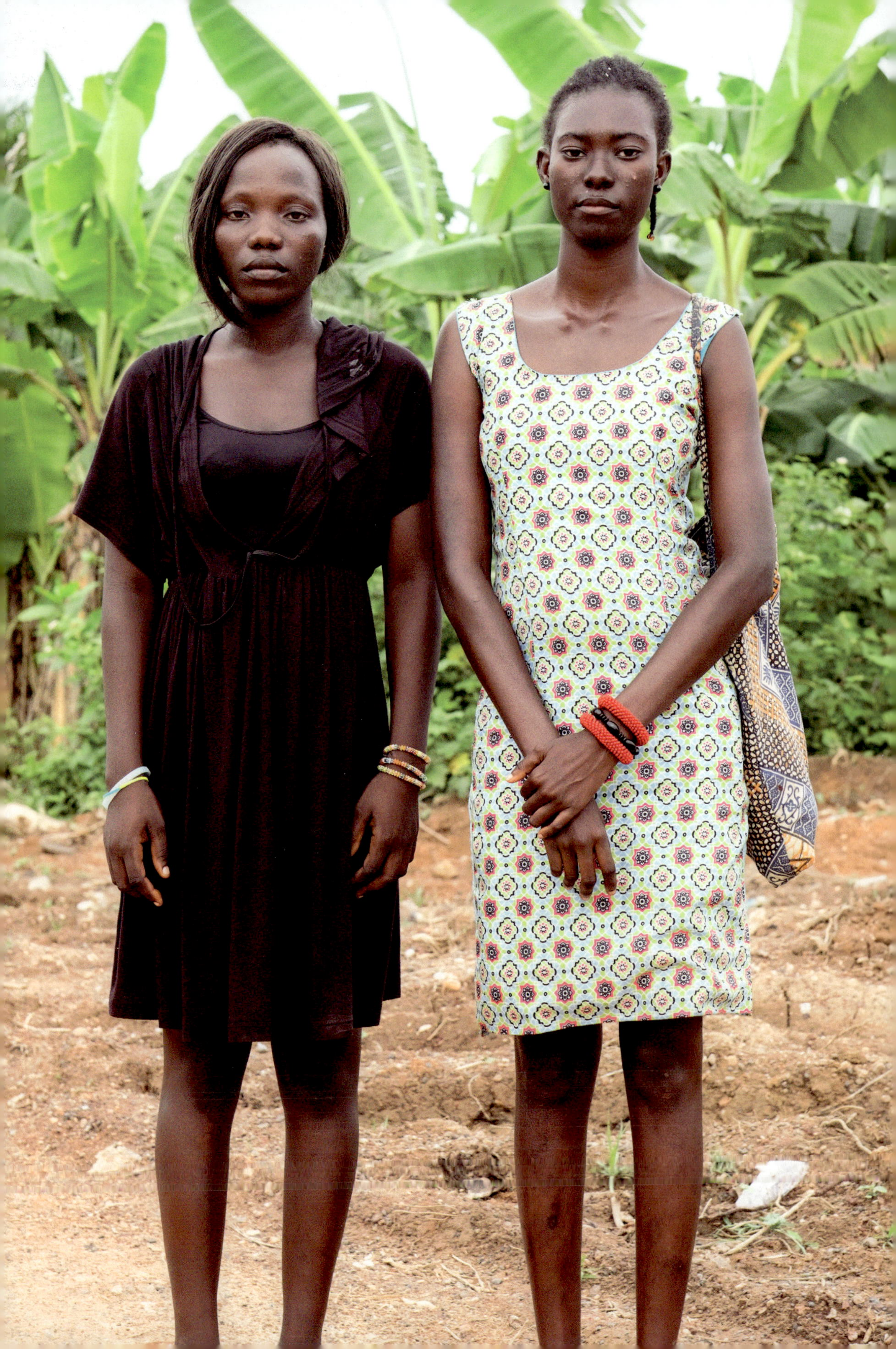

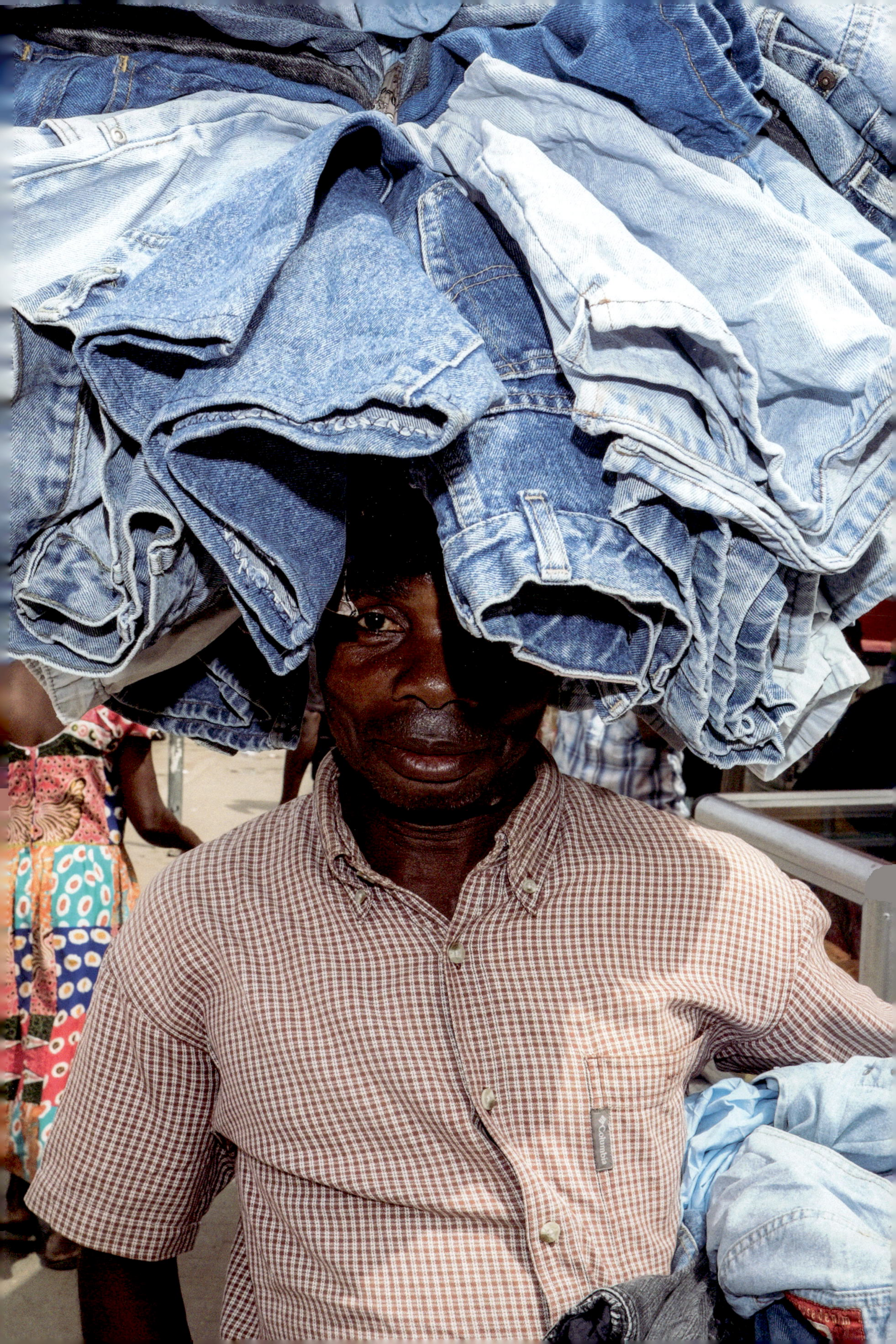
Columbia

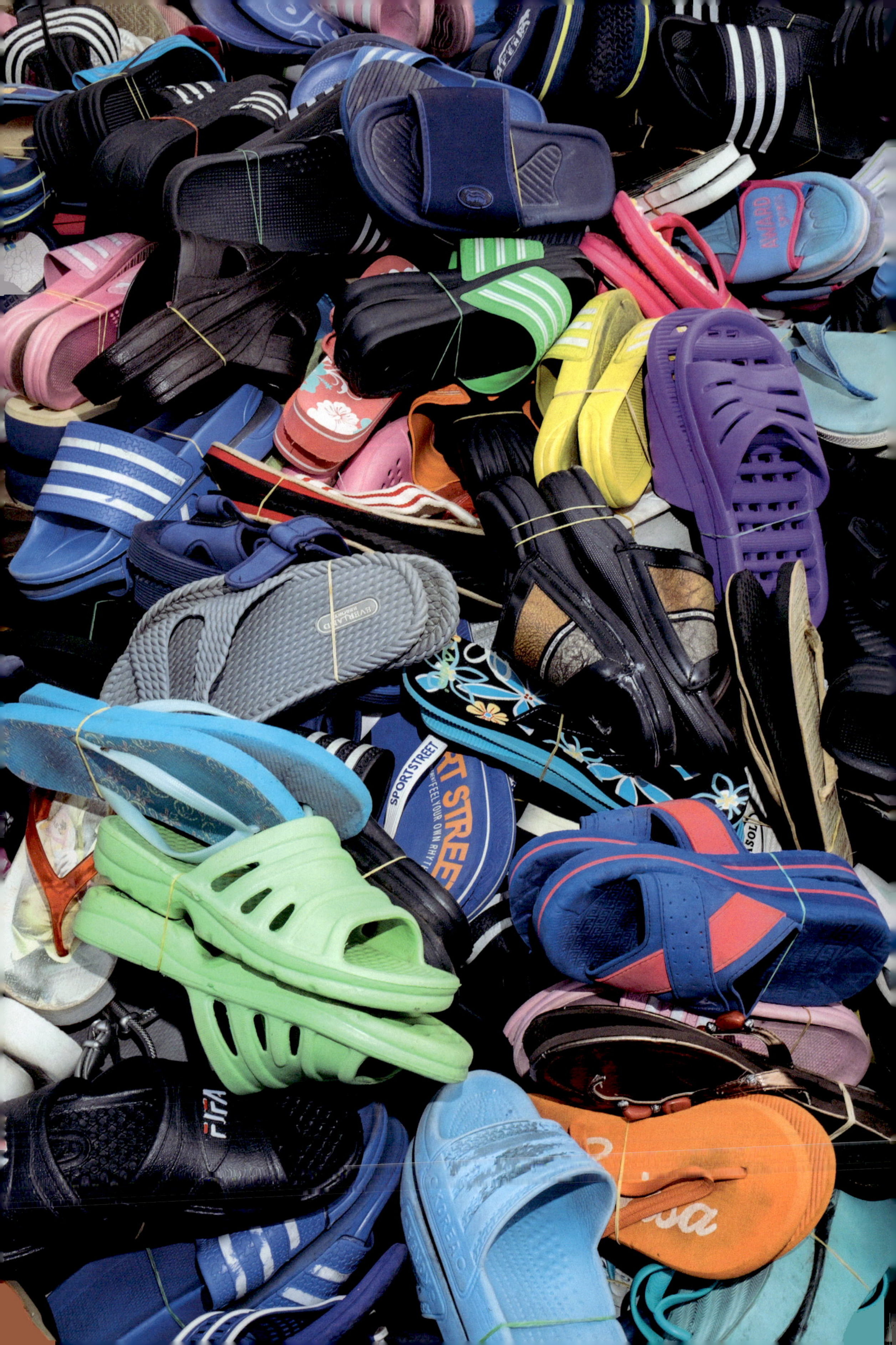
SPORTSTREET
AWARD

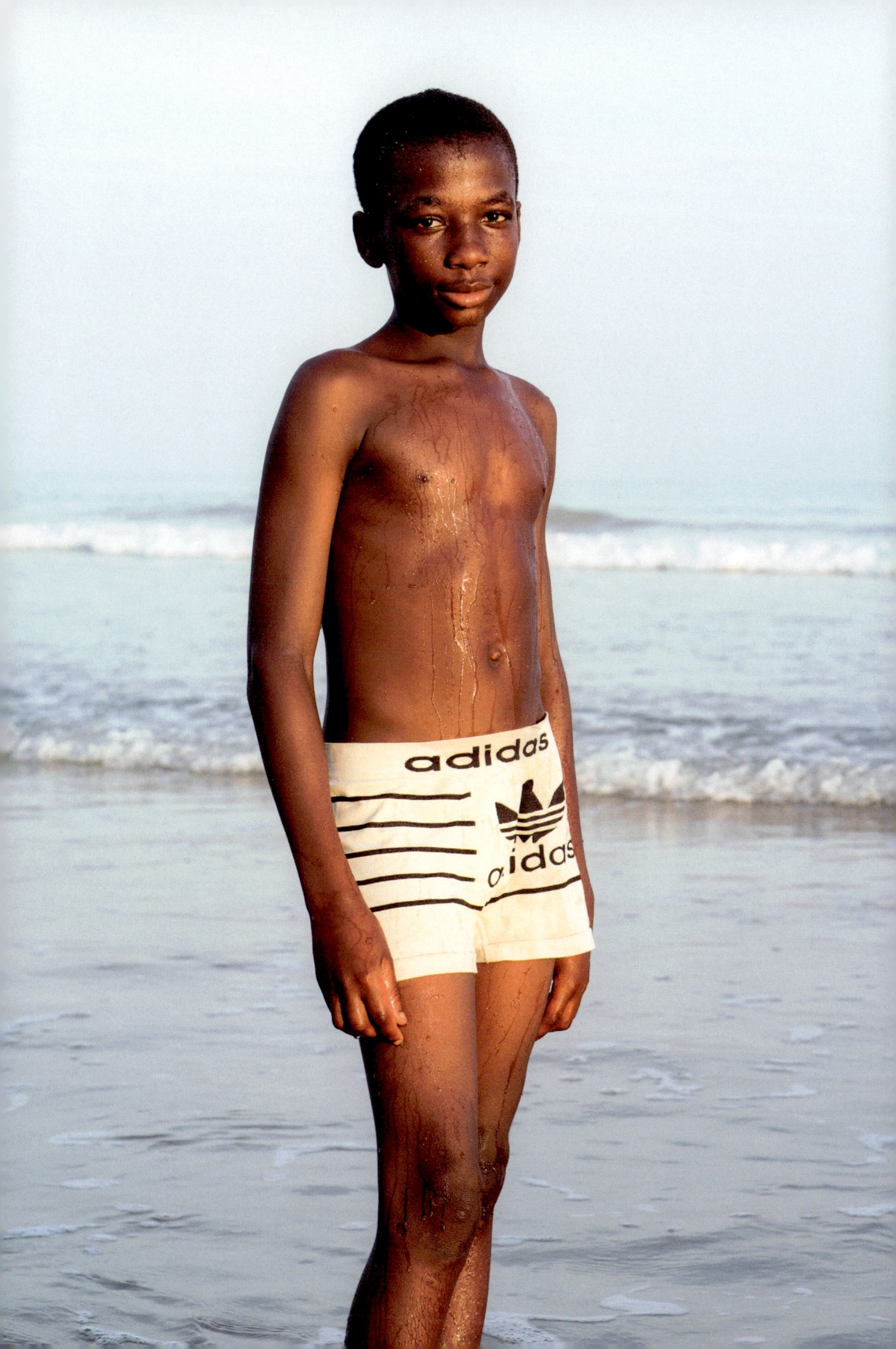
adidas
adidas

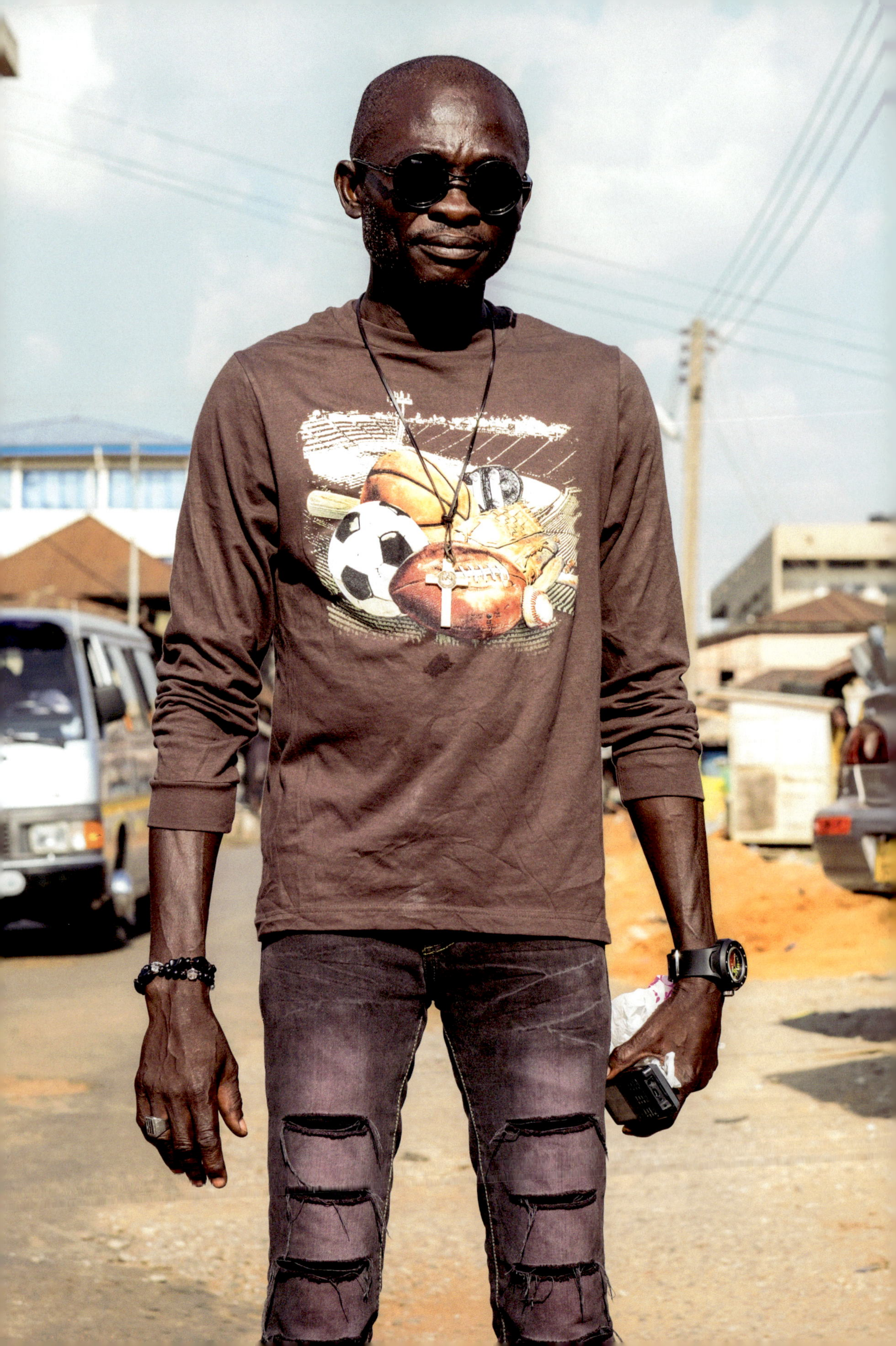

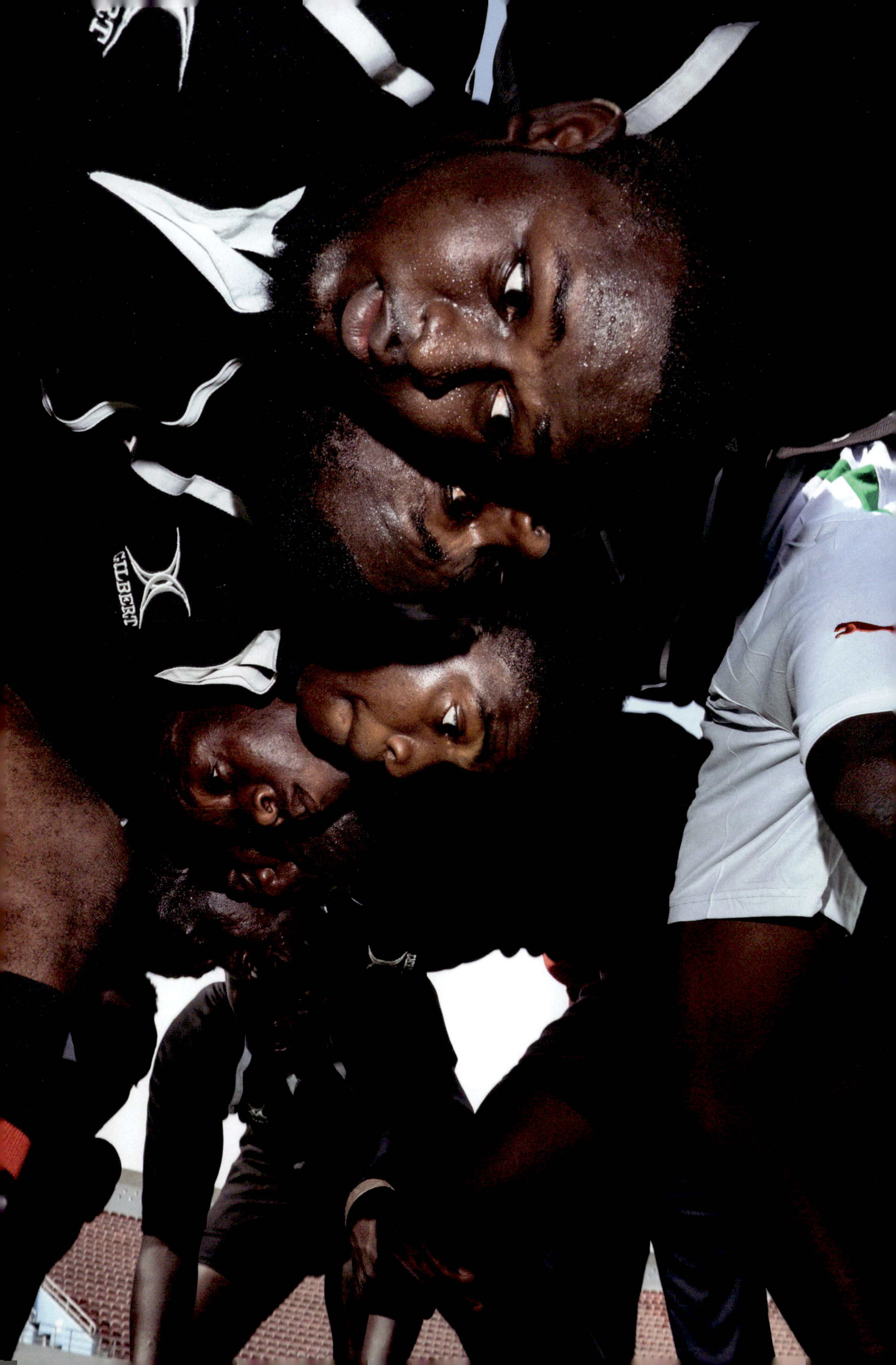
GILBERT

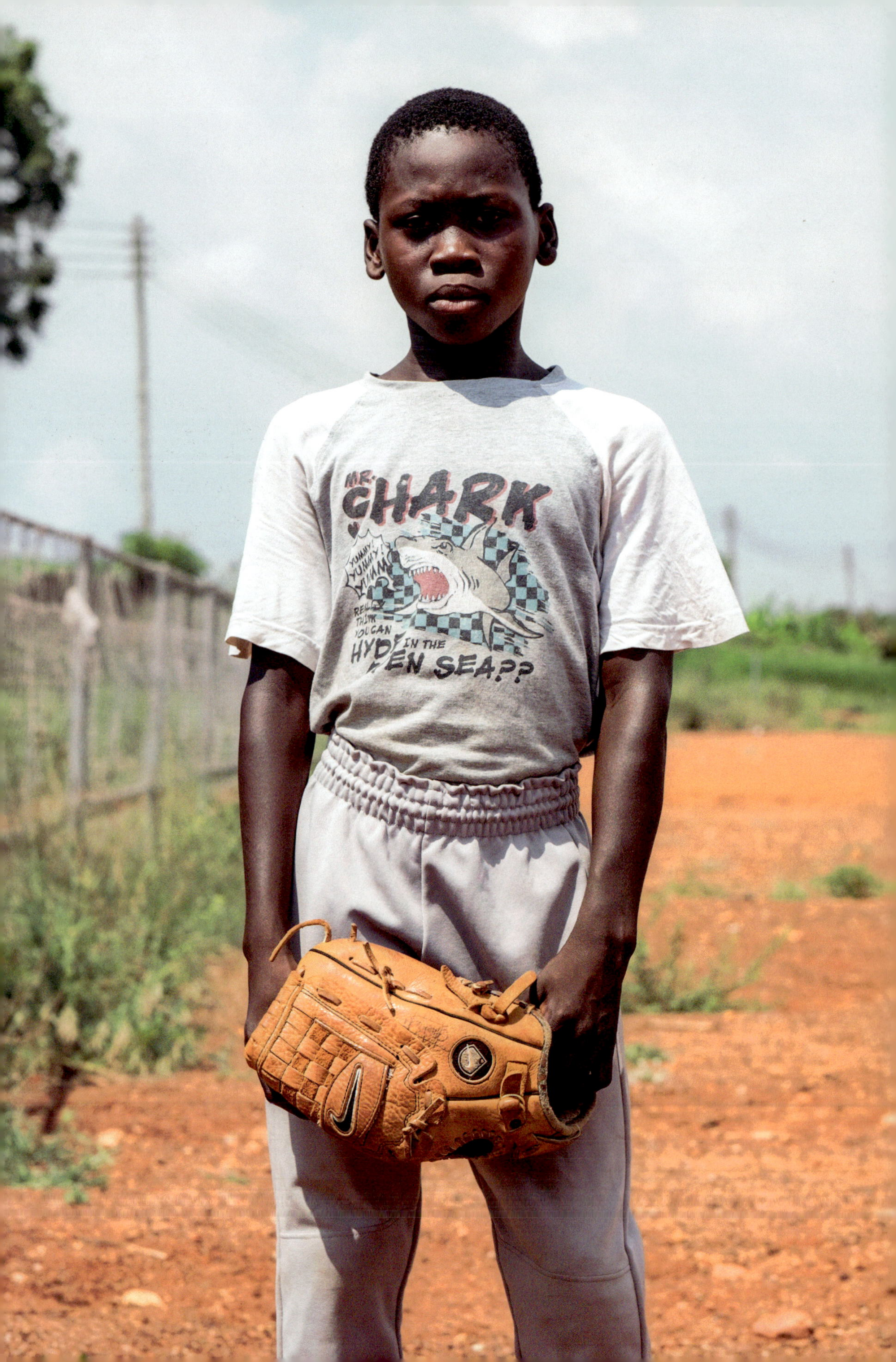
MR. CHARK
IN THE
EN SEA??

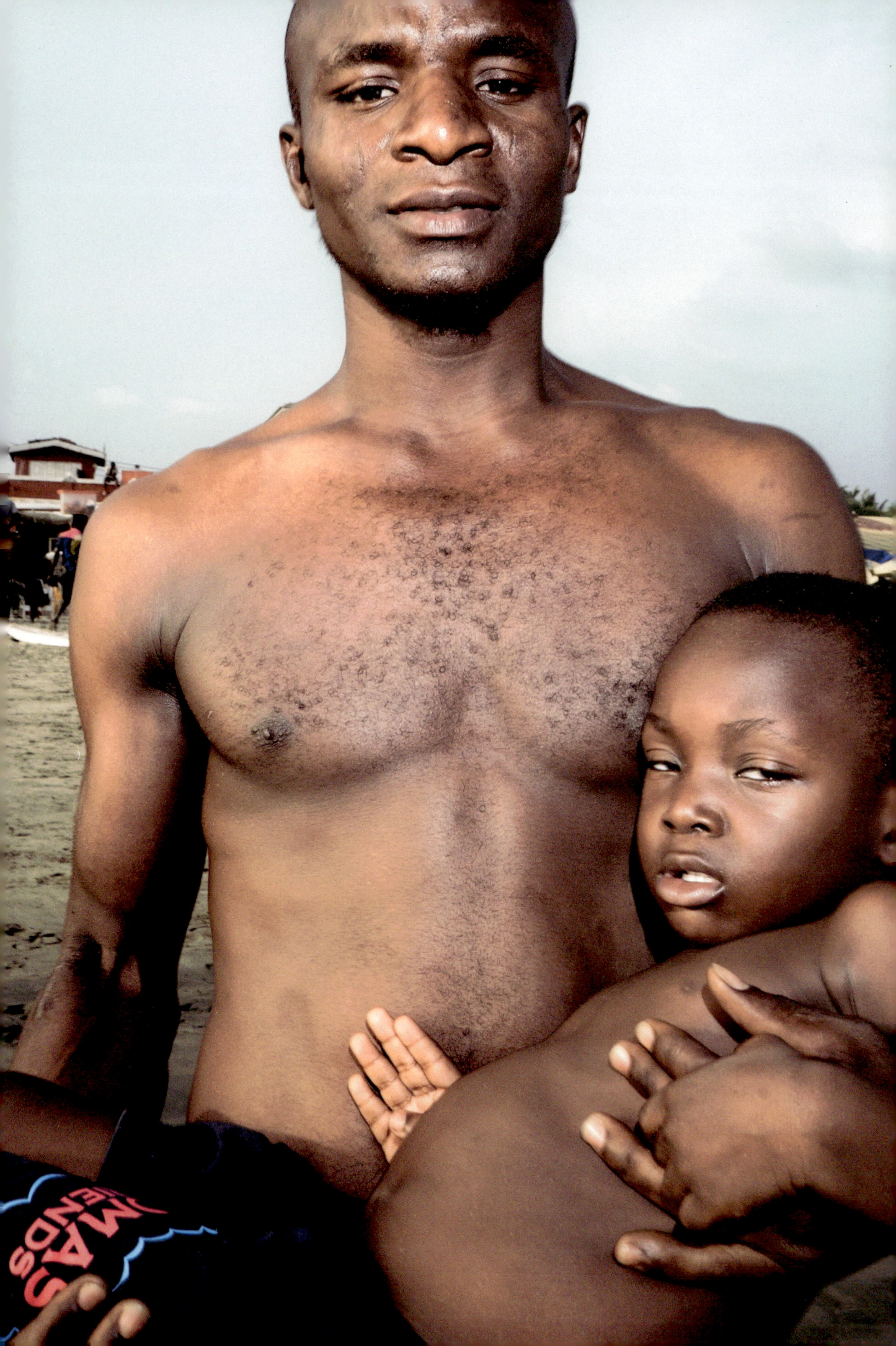

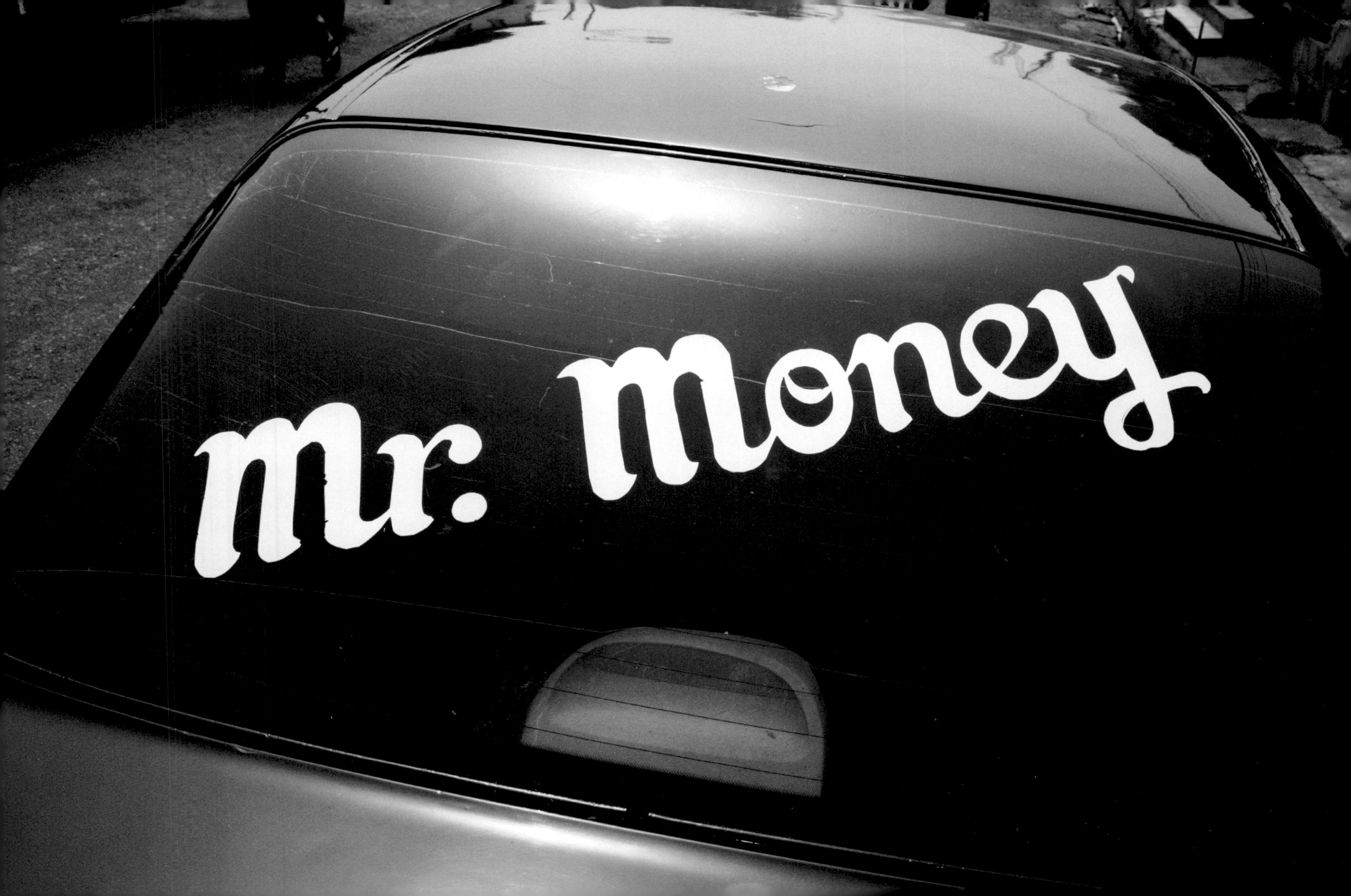
Mr. Money

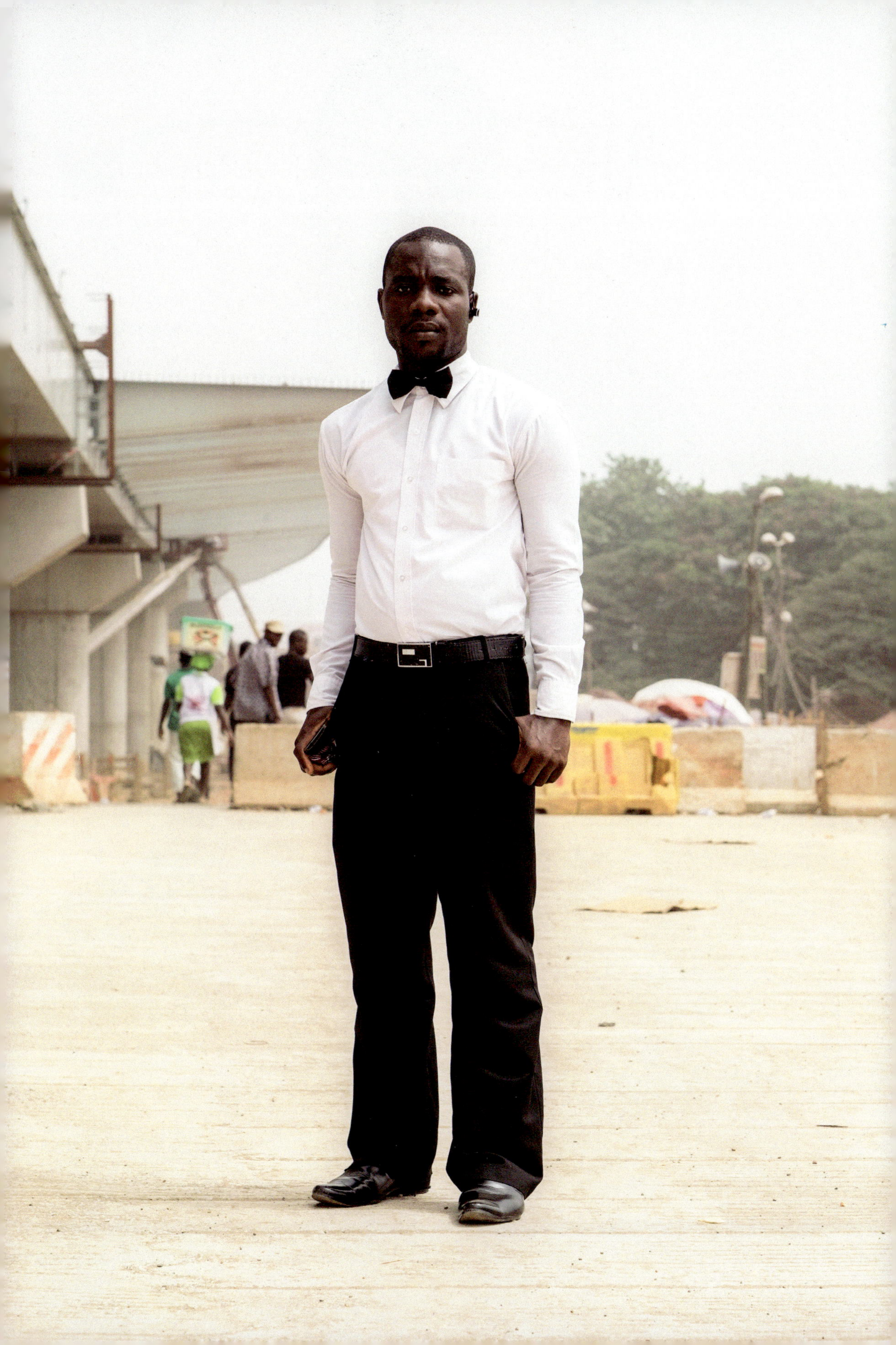

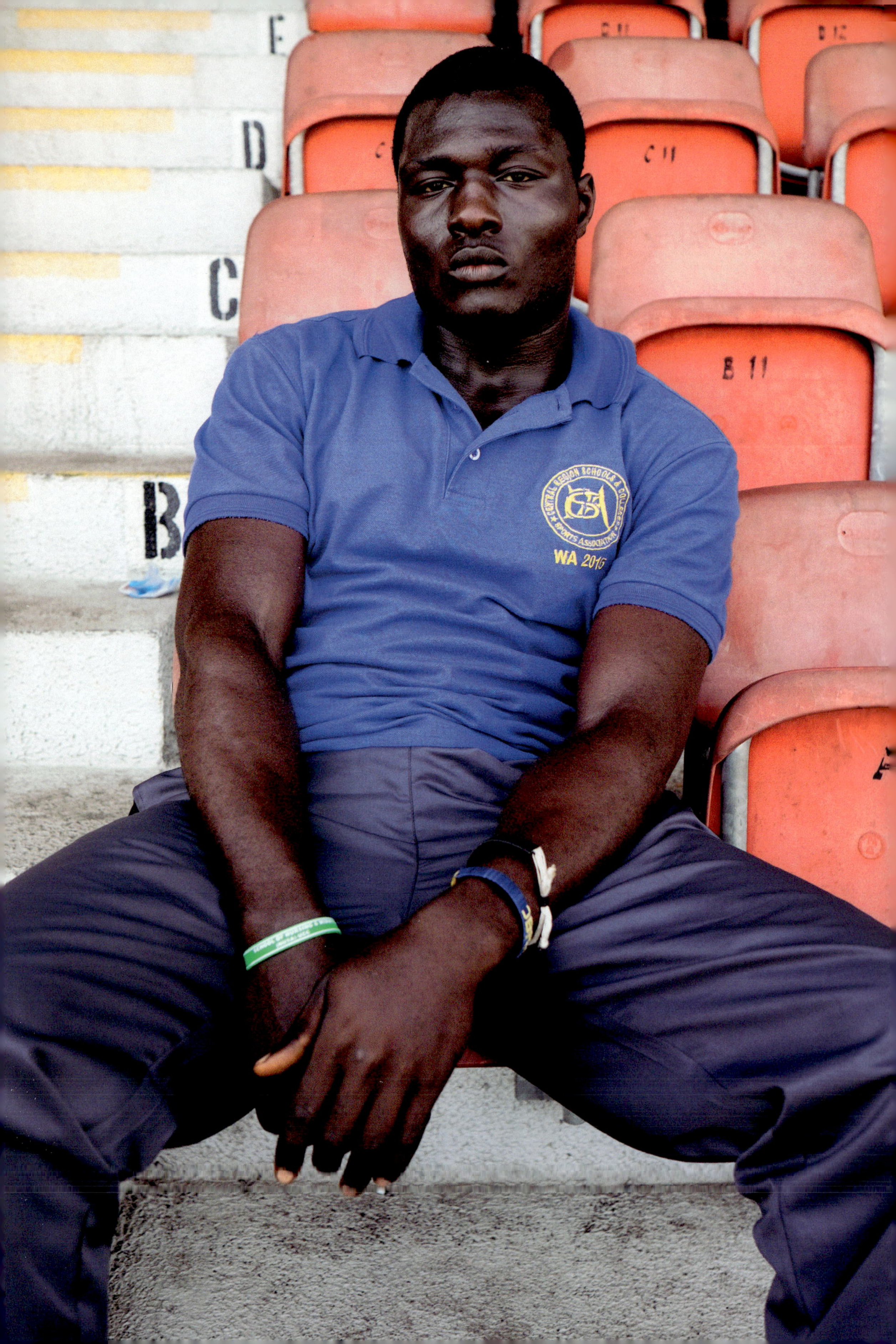
E
D
C
B
C 11
B 11
WA 2015

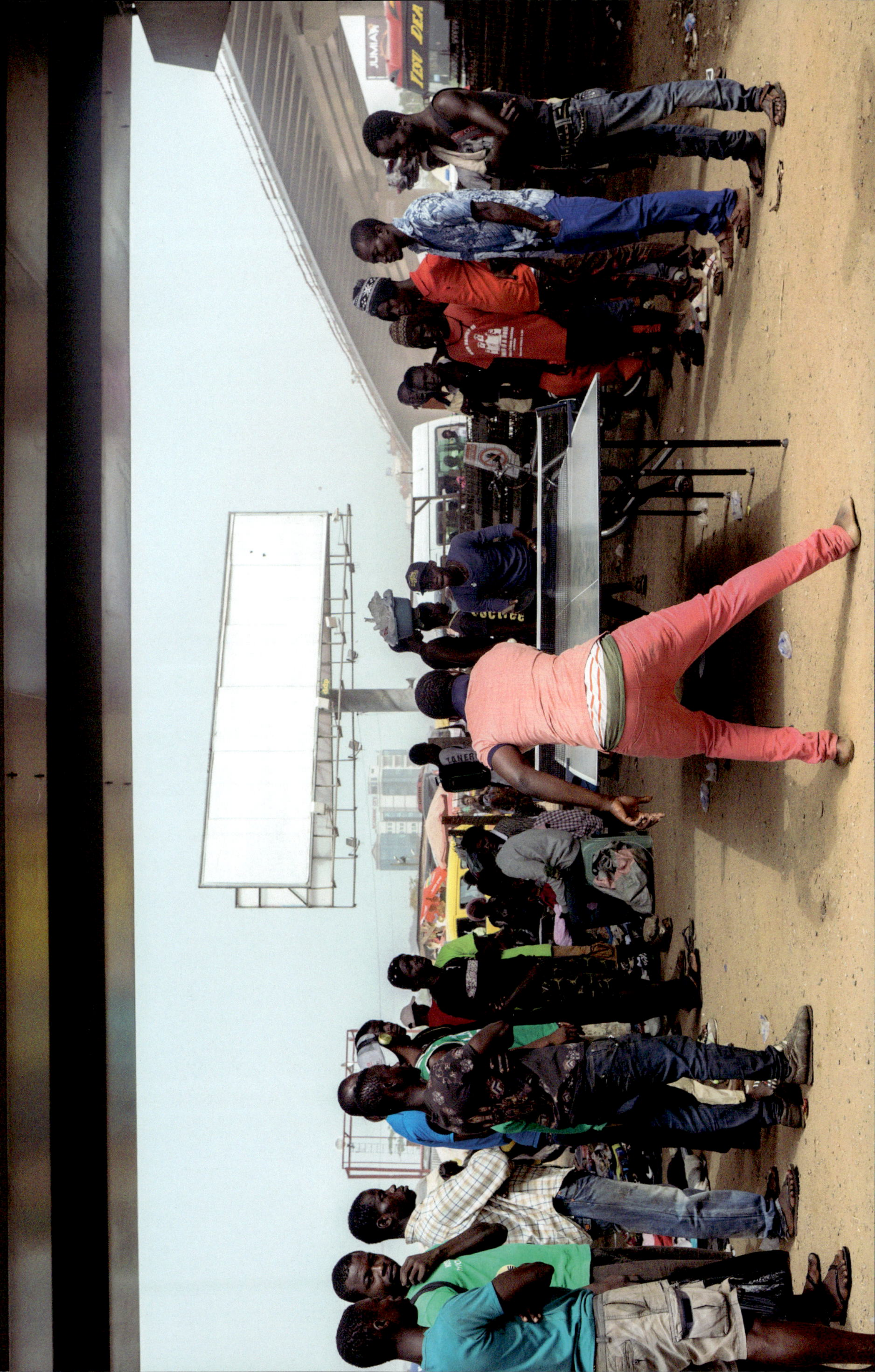

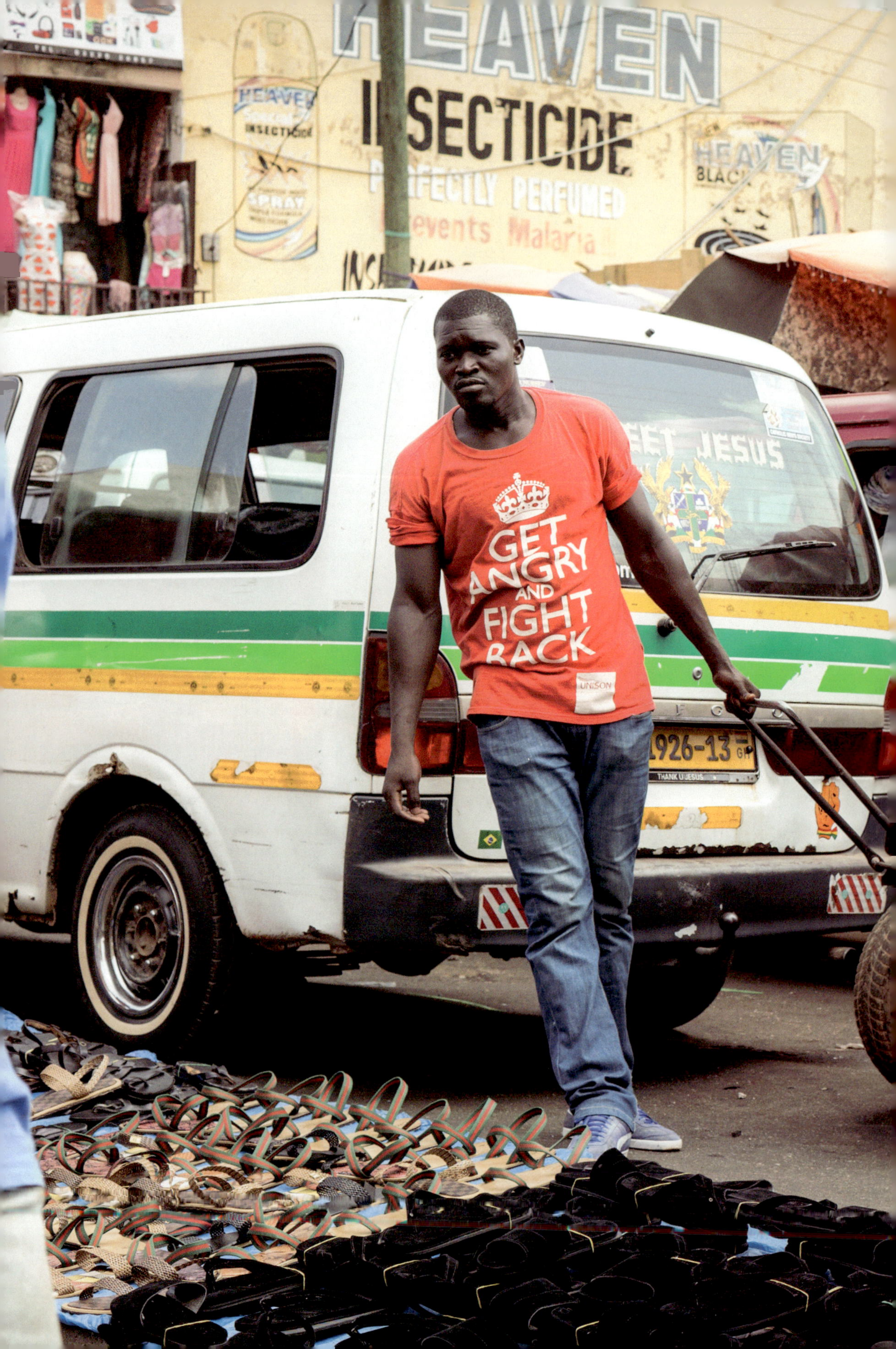
HEAVEN
GET ANGRY AND FIGHT BACK
UNISON
1926-13
THANK U JESUS

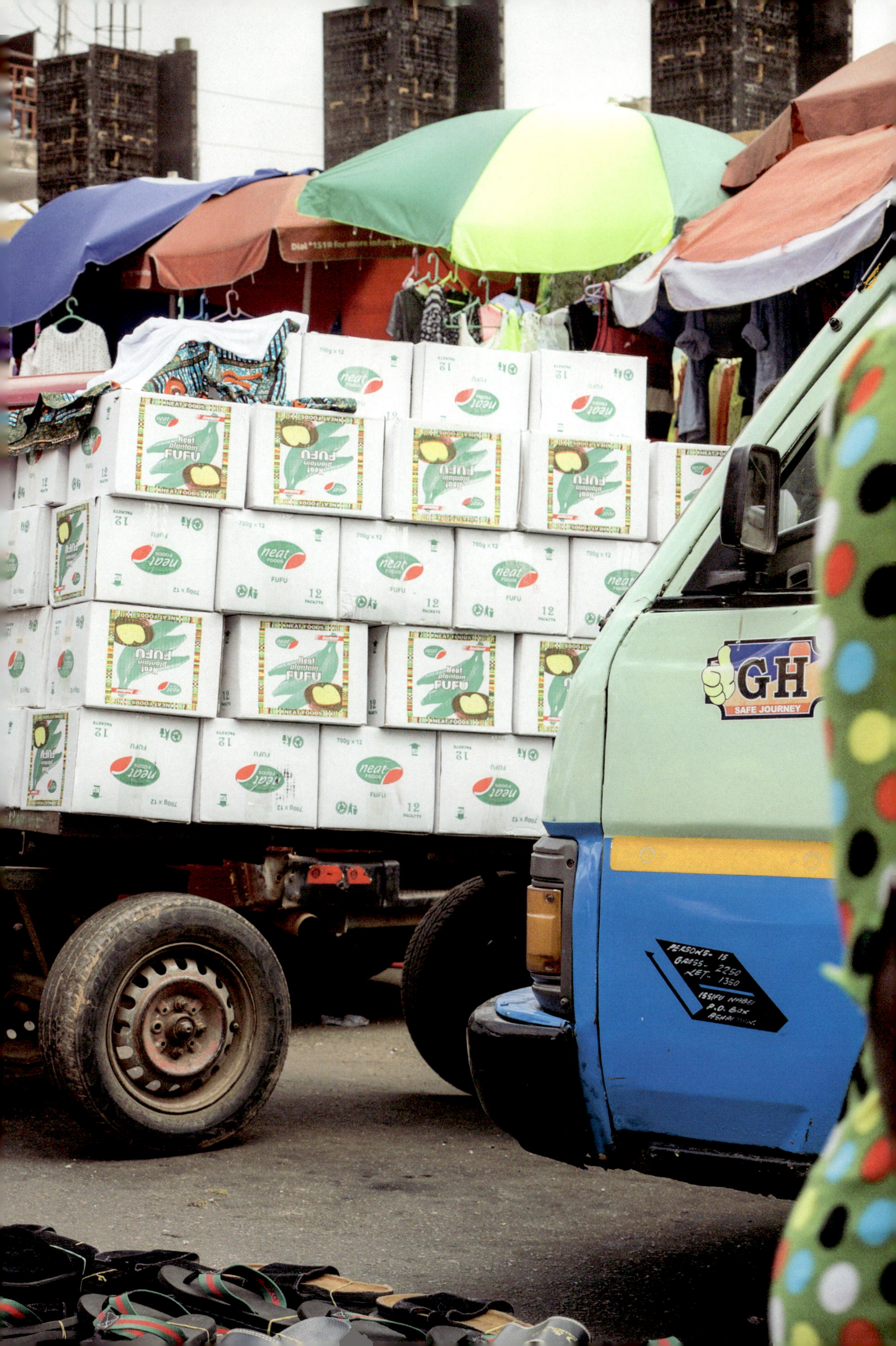
NEAT FOODS
Neat plantain FUFU
neat FOODS
FUFU
700g x 12
12 PACKETS
GH
SAFE JOURNEY
PERSONS- 15
GROSS- 2250
LET- 1350
ISSIFU NABEI
P.O. BOX

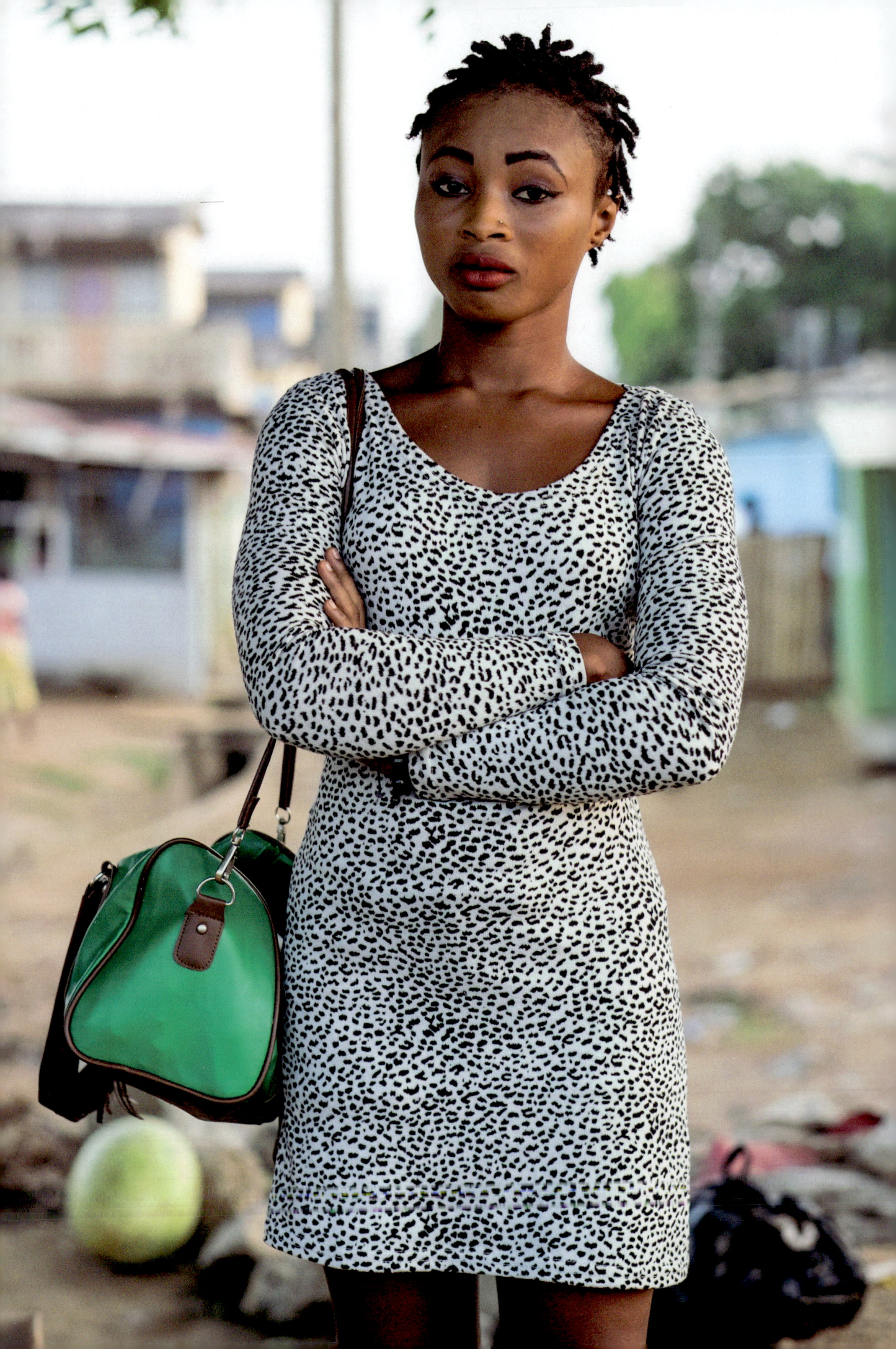

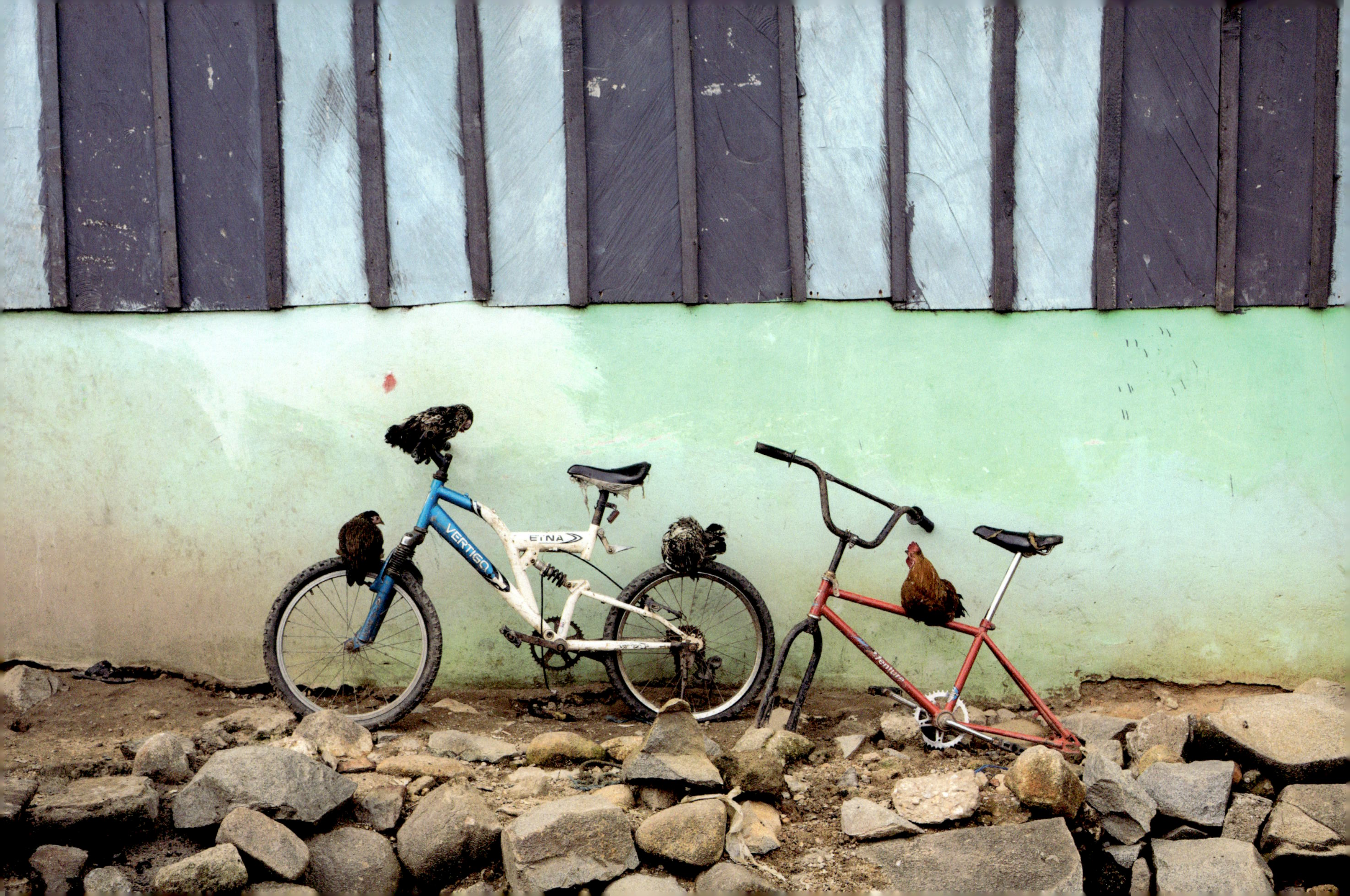
VERTIGO
ETNA

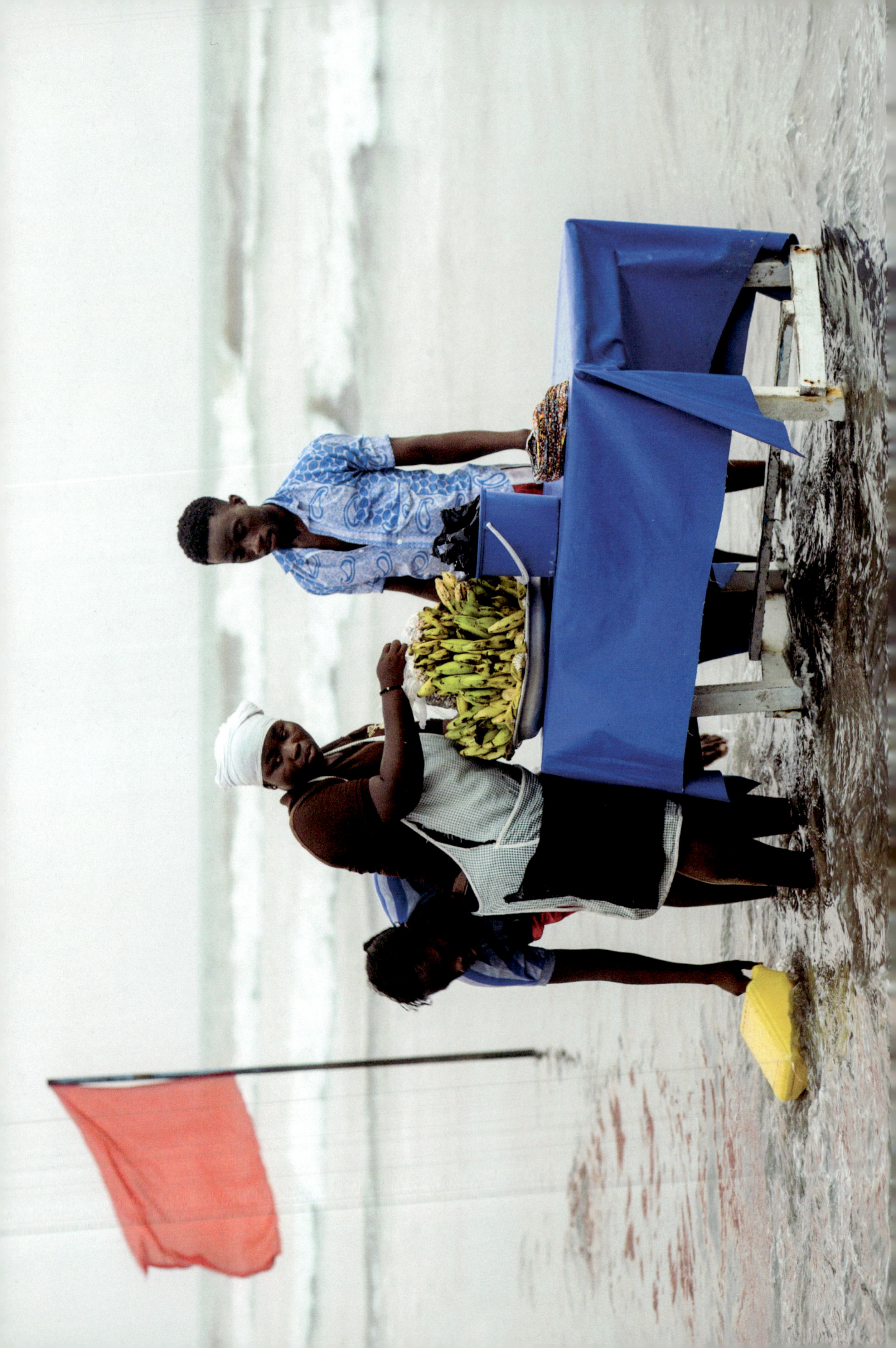

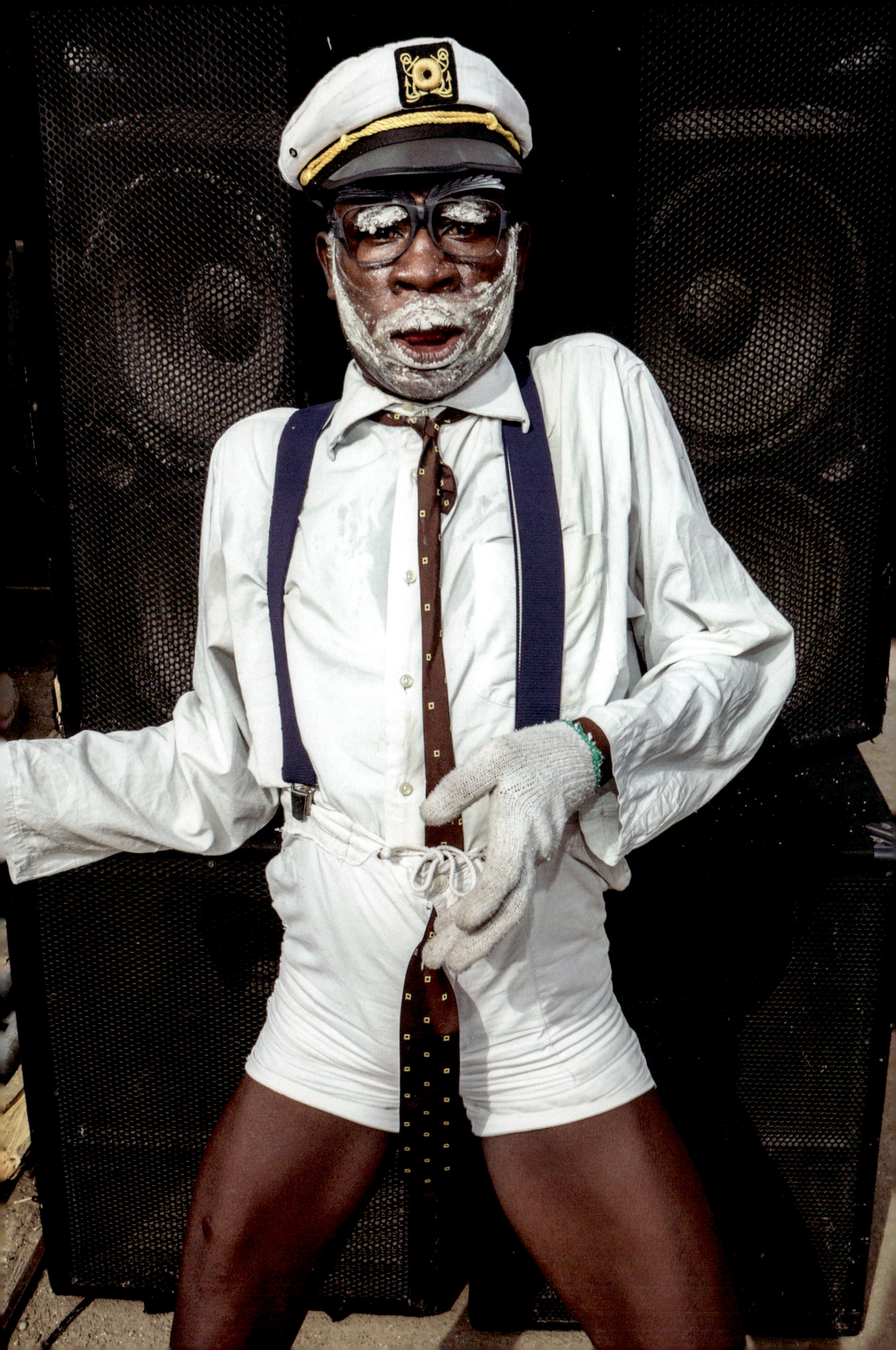

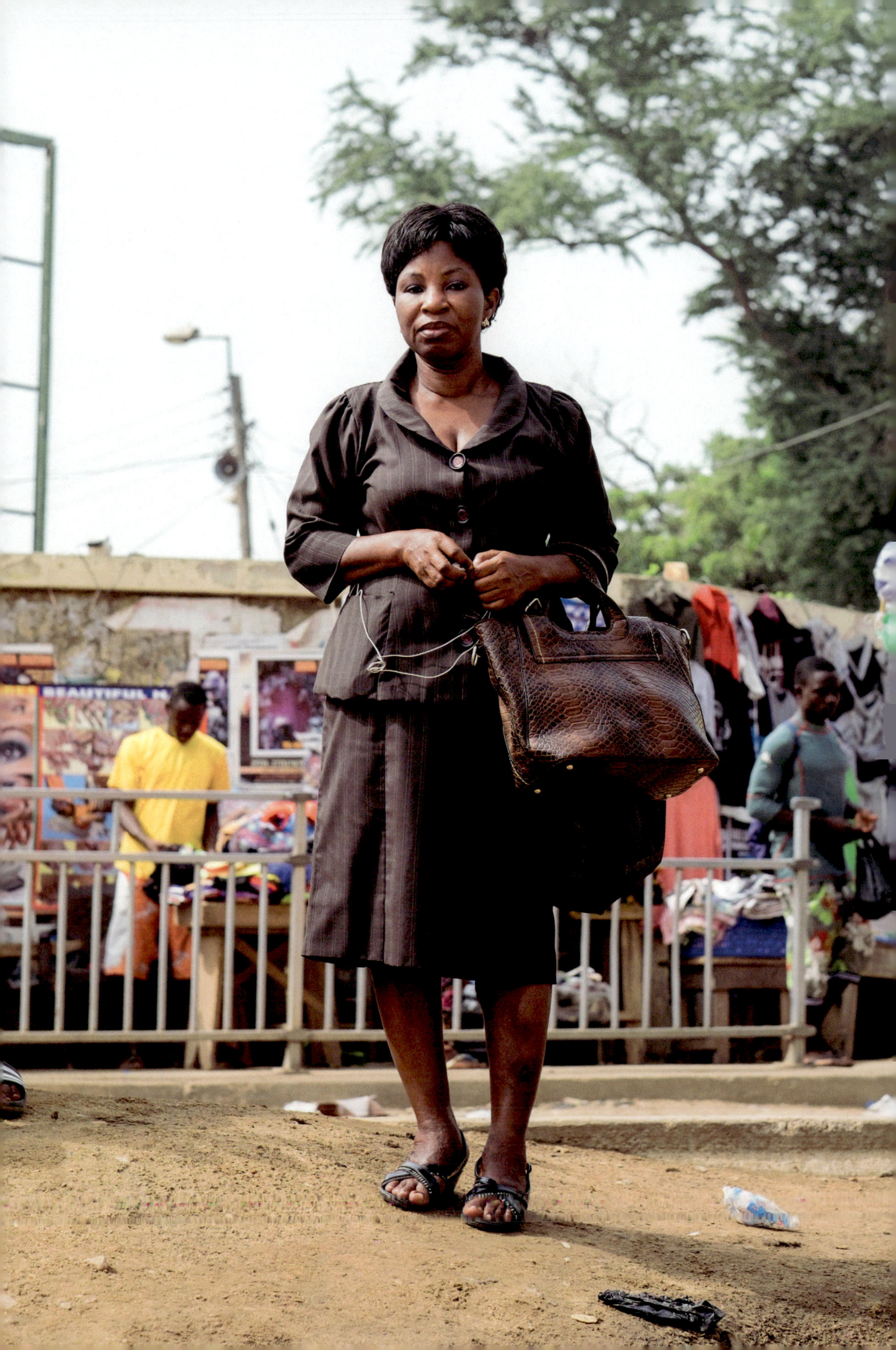
BEAUTIFUL

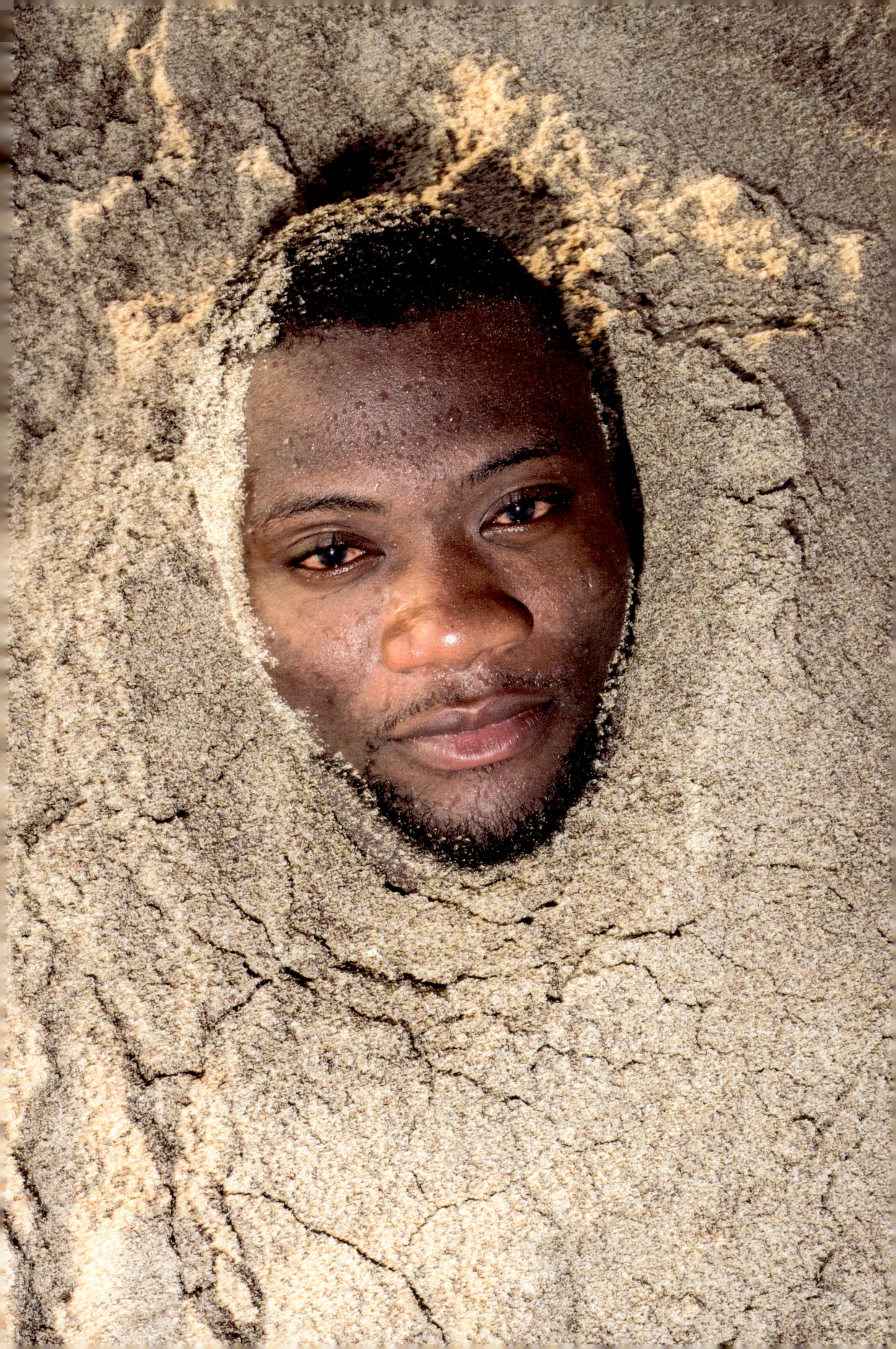

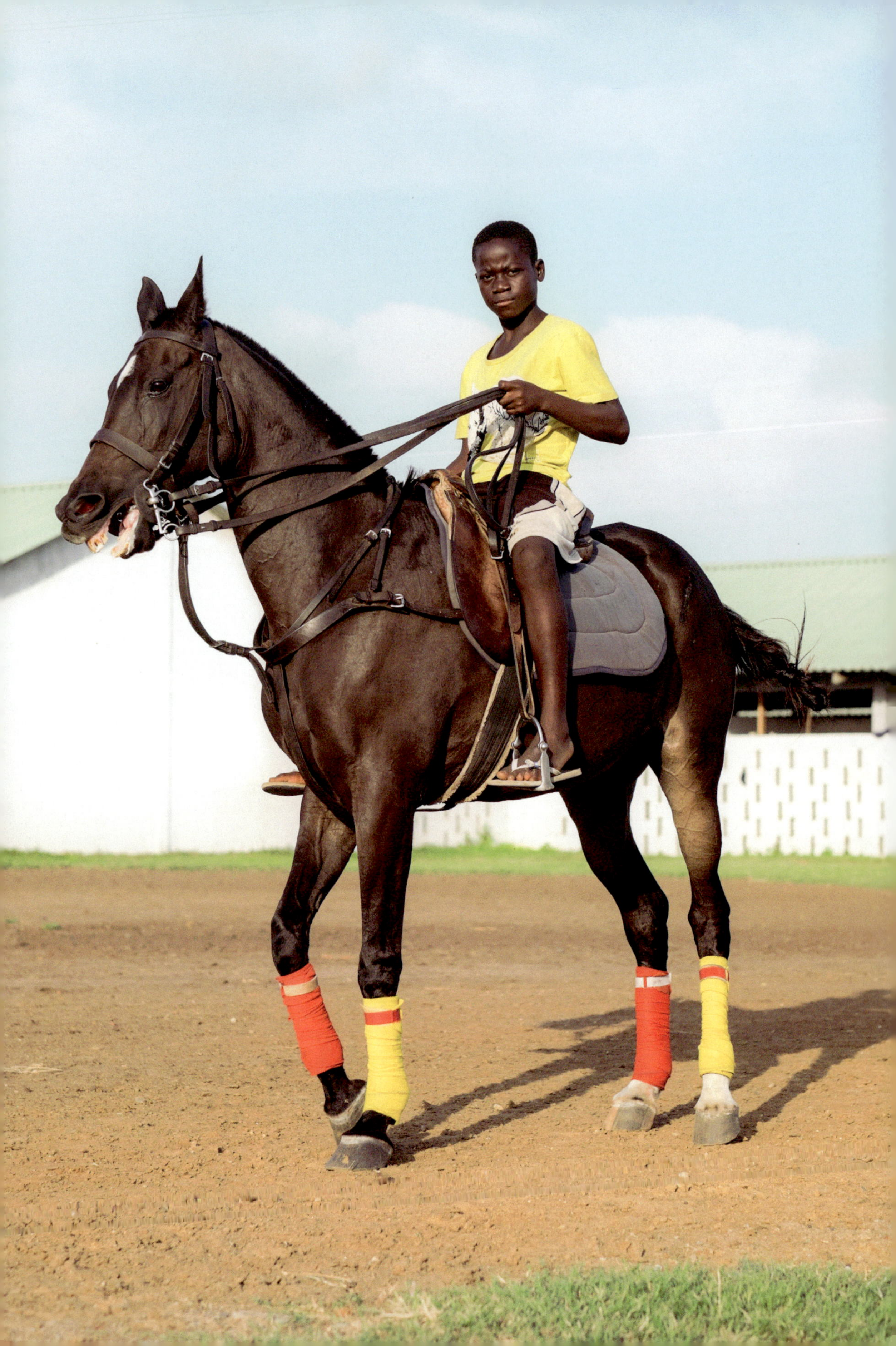

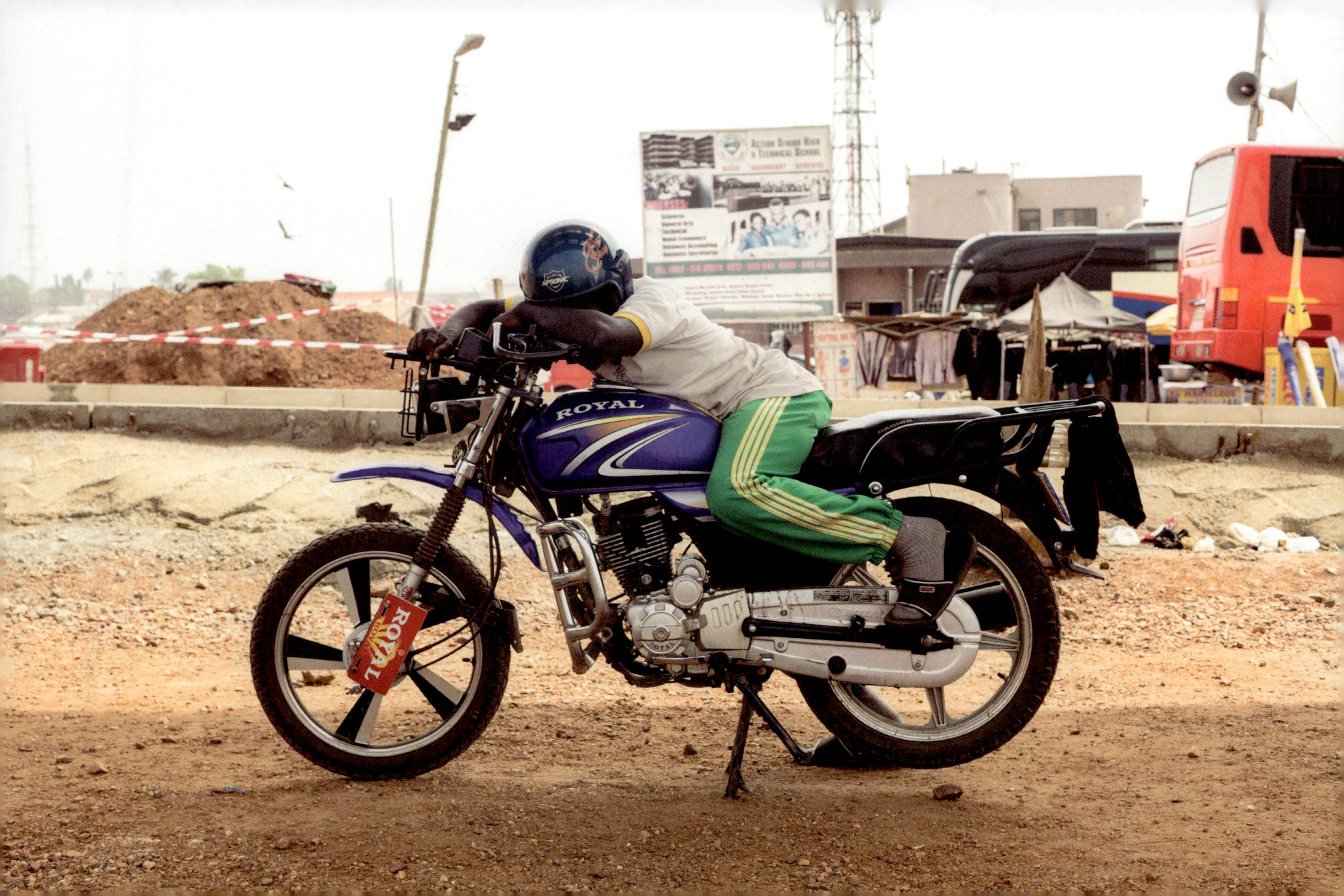
ACTION SENIOR HIGH
& TECHNICAL SCHOOL
APSONIC
ROYAL
ROYAL

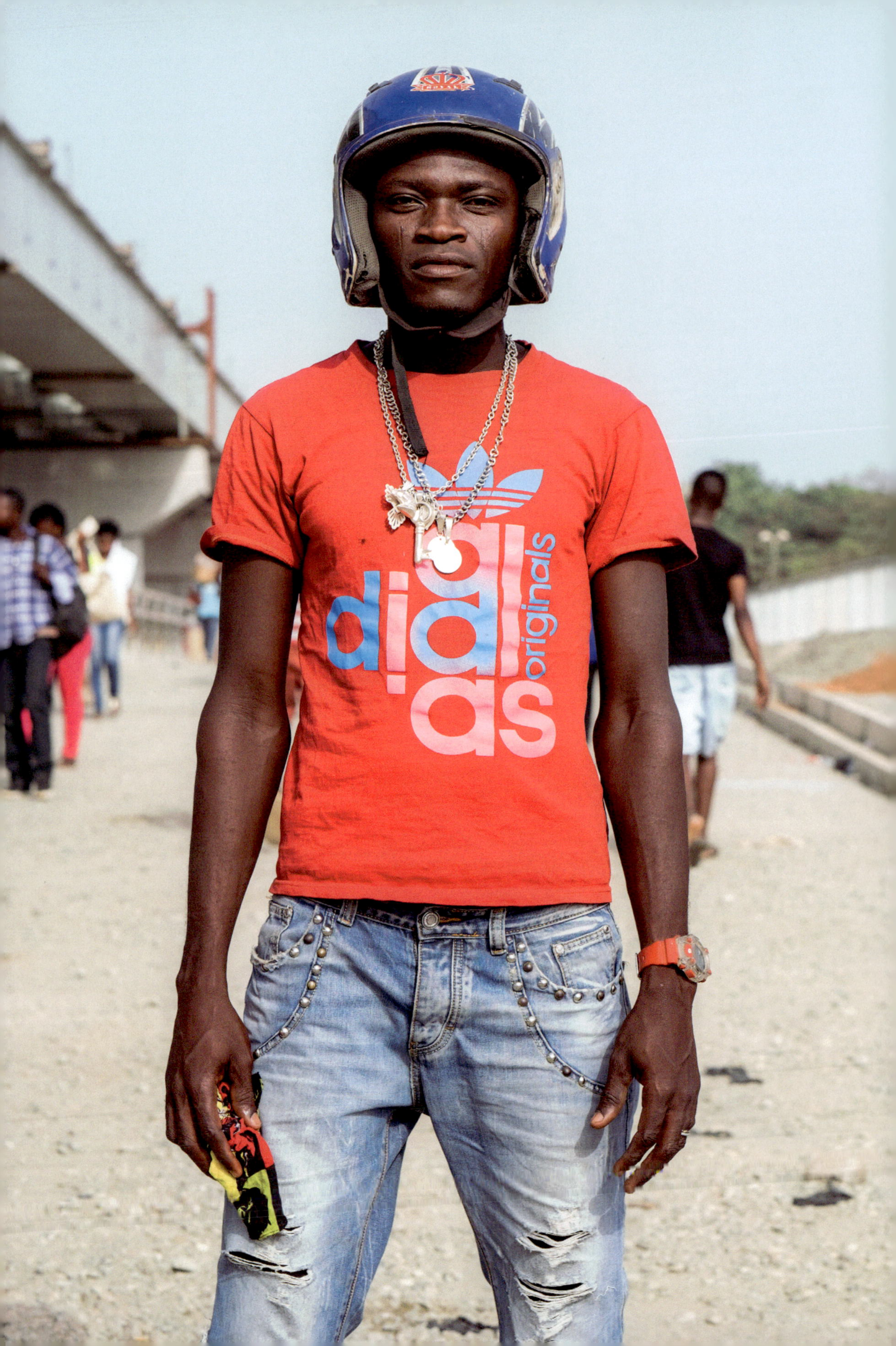
originals

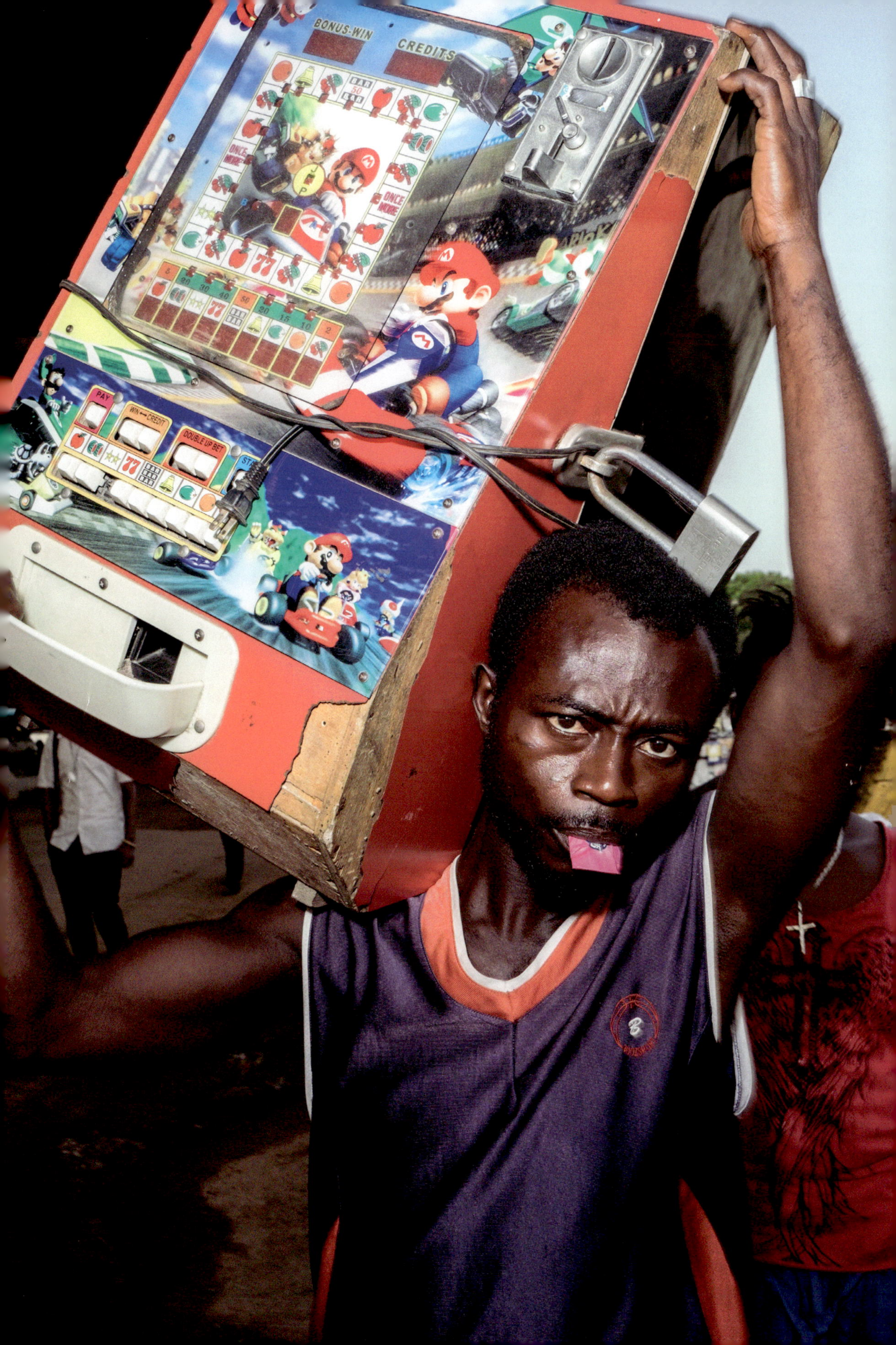
BONUS-WIN
CREDITS
ONCE MORE
ONCE MORE
PAY
WIN CREDIT
DOUBLE UP BET

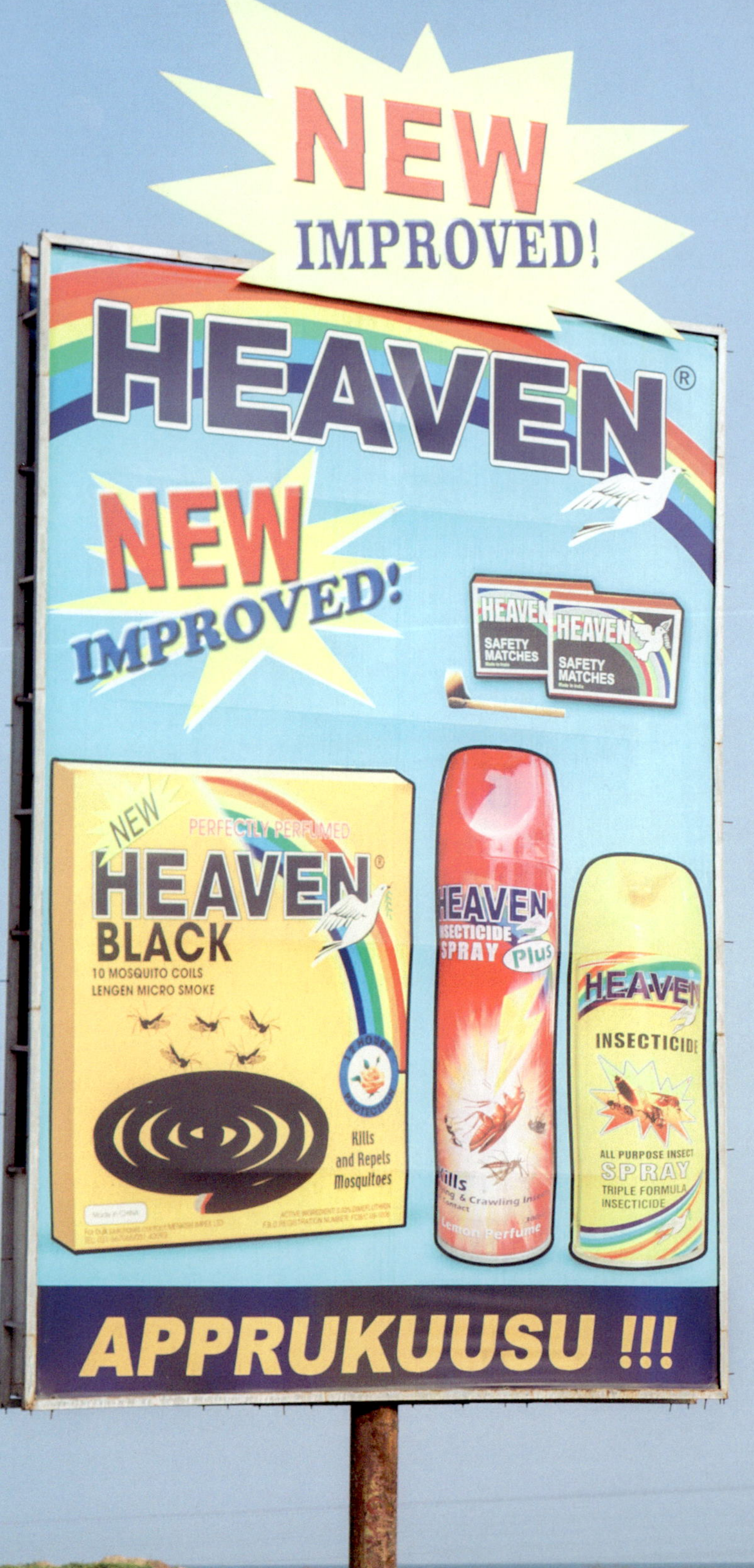
NEW
IMPROVED!
HEAVEN®
NEW
IMPROVED!
HEAVEN
SAFETY MATCHES
HEAVEN
SAFETY MATCHES
NEW
PERFECTLY PERFUMED
HEAVEN®
BLACK
10 MOSQUITO COILS
LENGEN MICRO SMOKE
Kills
and Repels
Mosquitoes
HEAVEN
INSECTICIDE
SPRAY
Plus
Lemon Perfume
HEAVEN
INSECTICIDE
ALL PURPOSE INSECT
SPRAY
TRIPLE FORMULA
INSECTICIDE
APPRUKUUSU !!!

KEEP OFF
DUMPING OF
REFUSE HERE IS
PROHIBITED

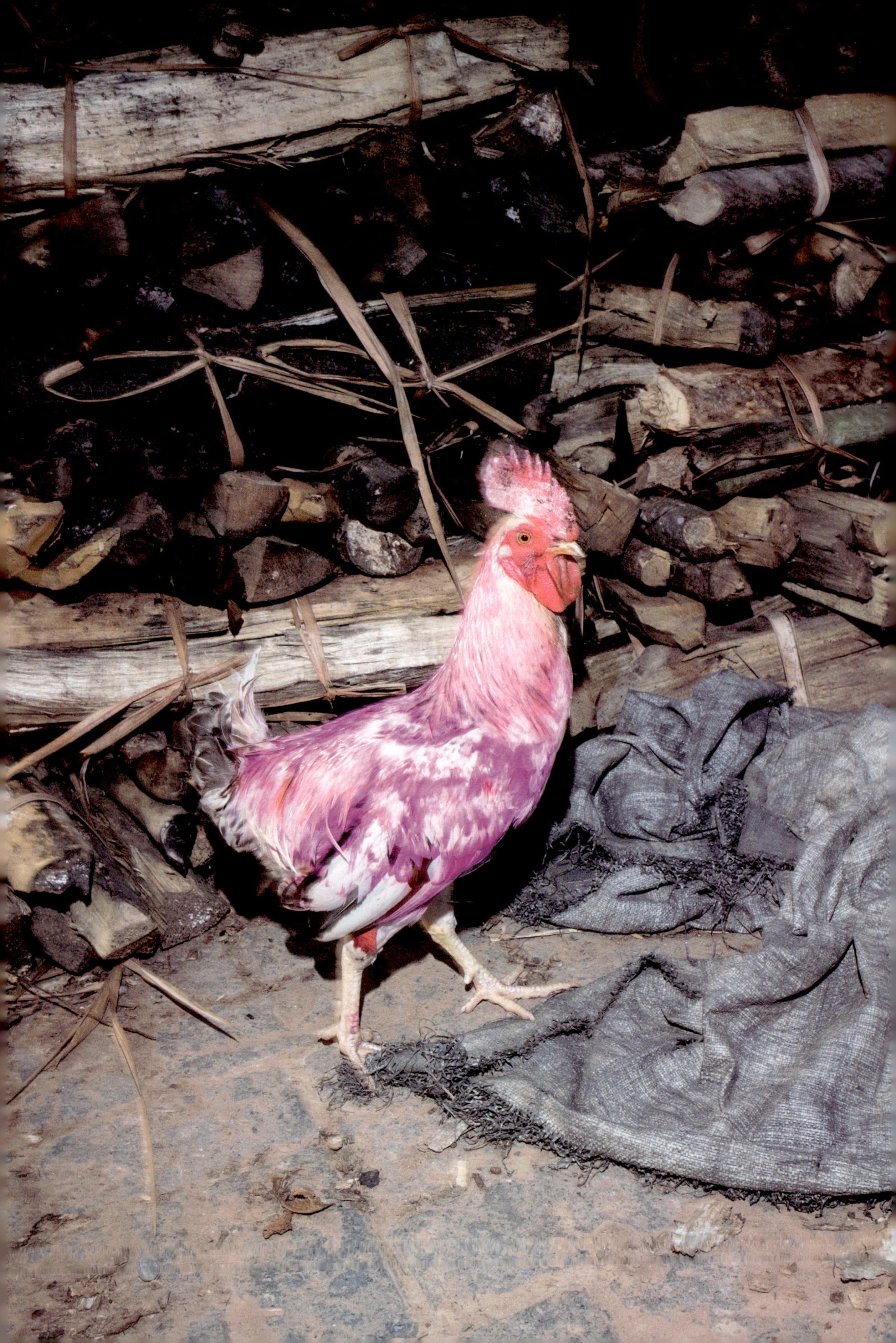

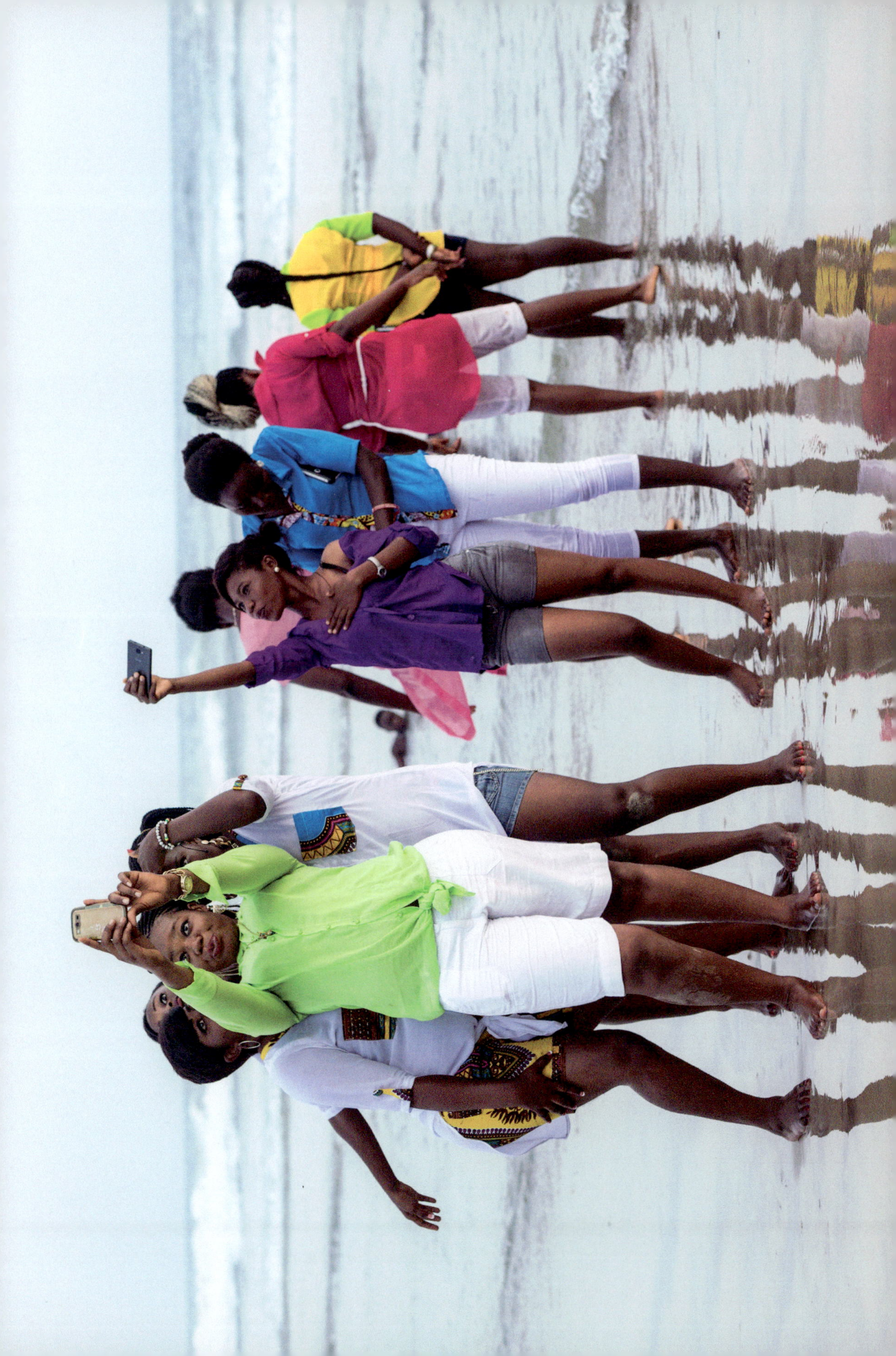

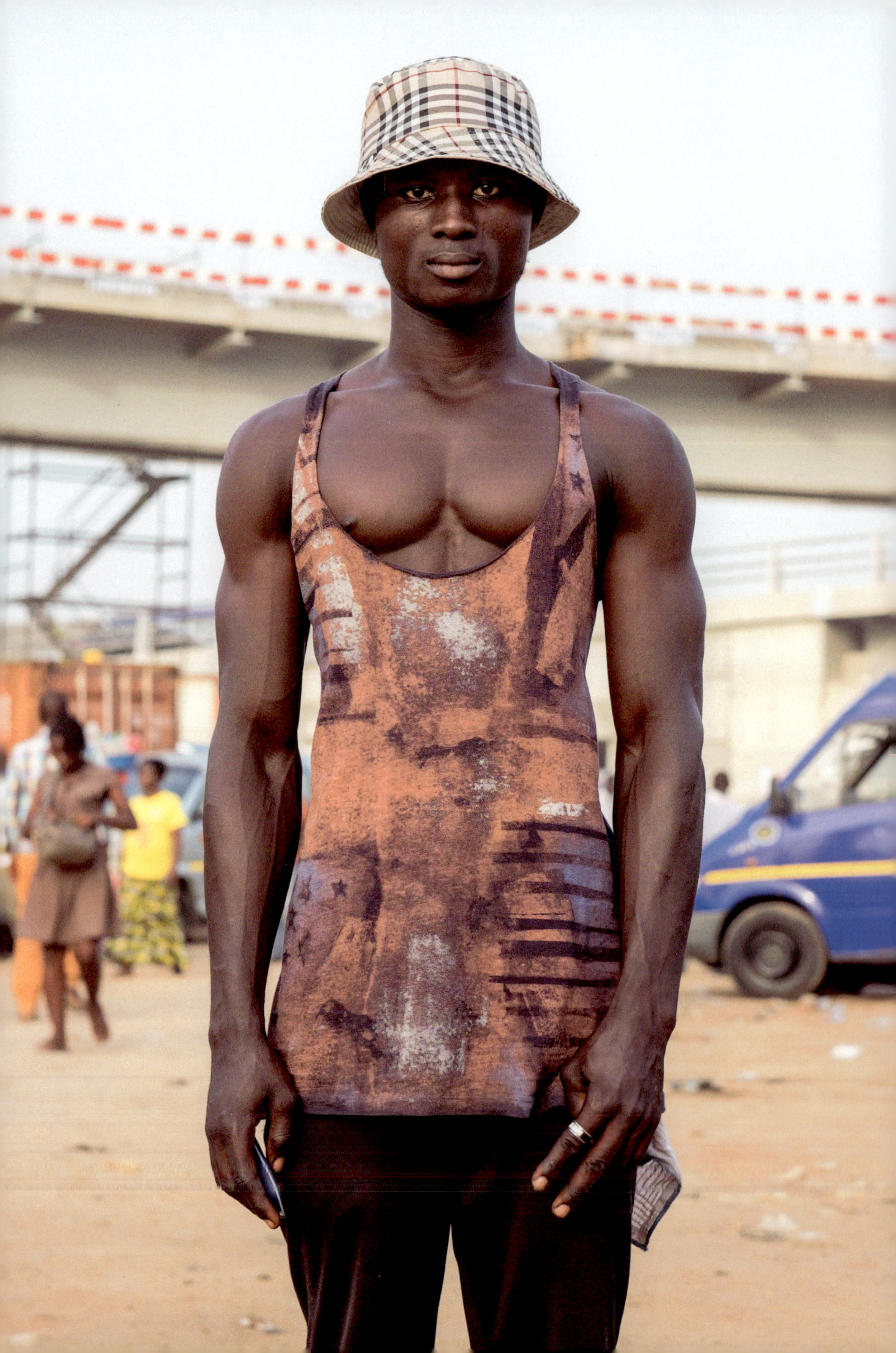

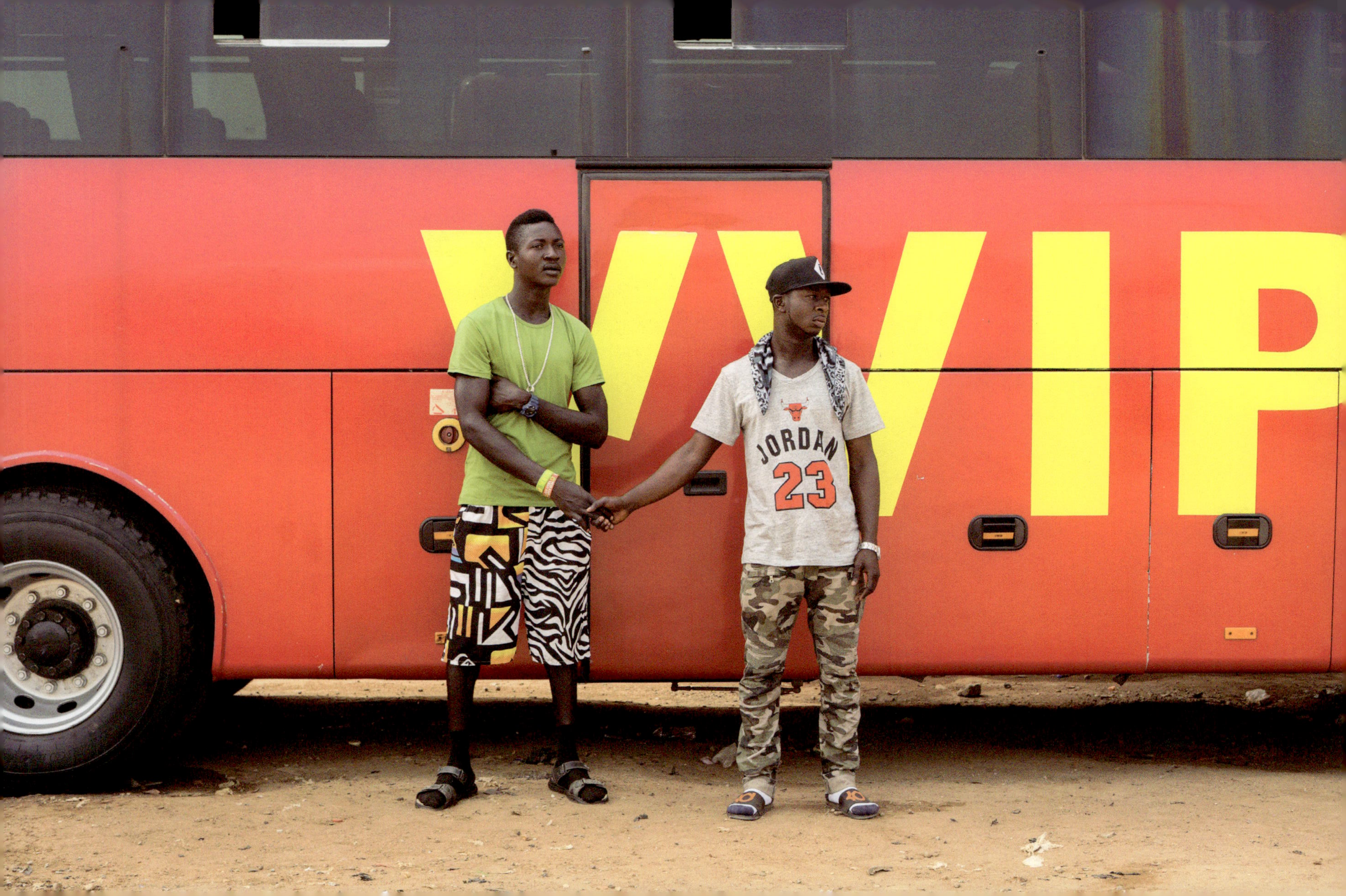
VVIP
JORDAN
23

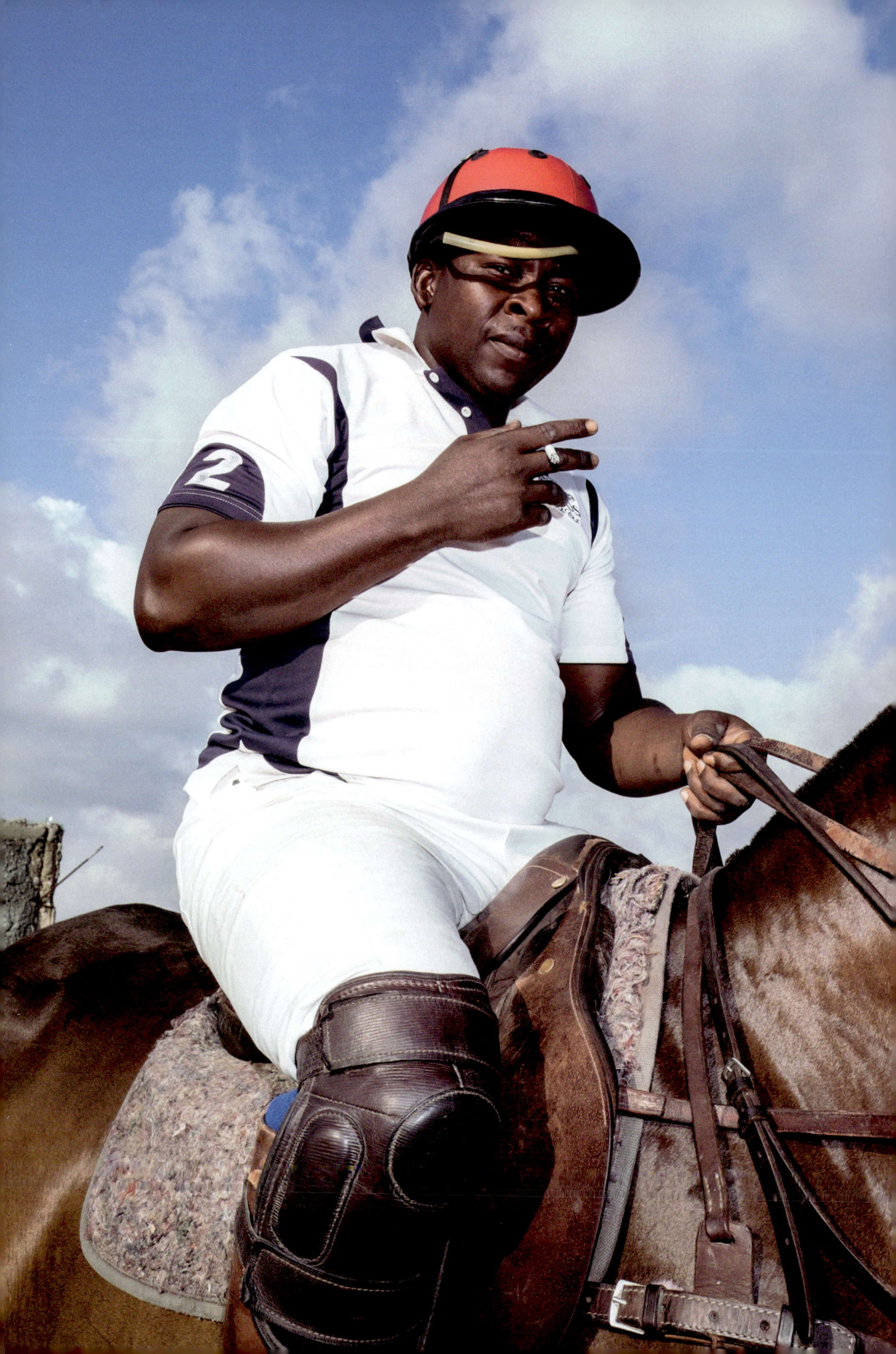
2

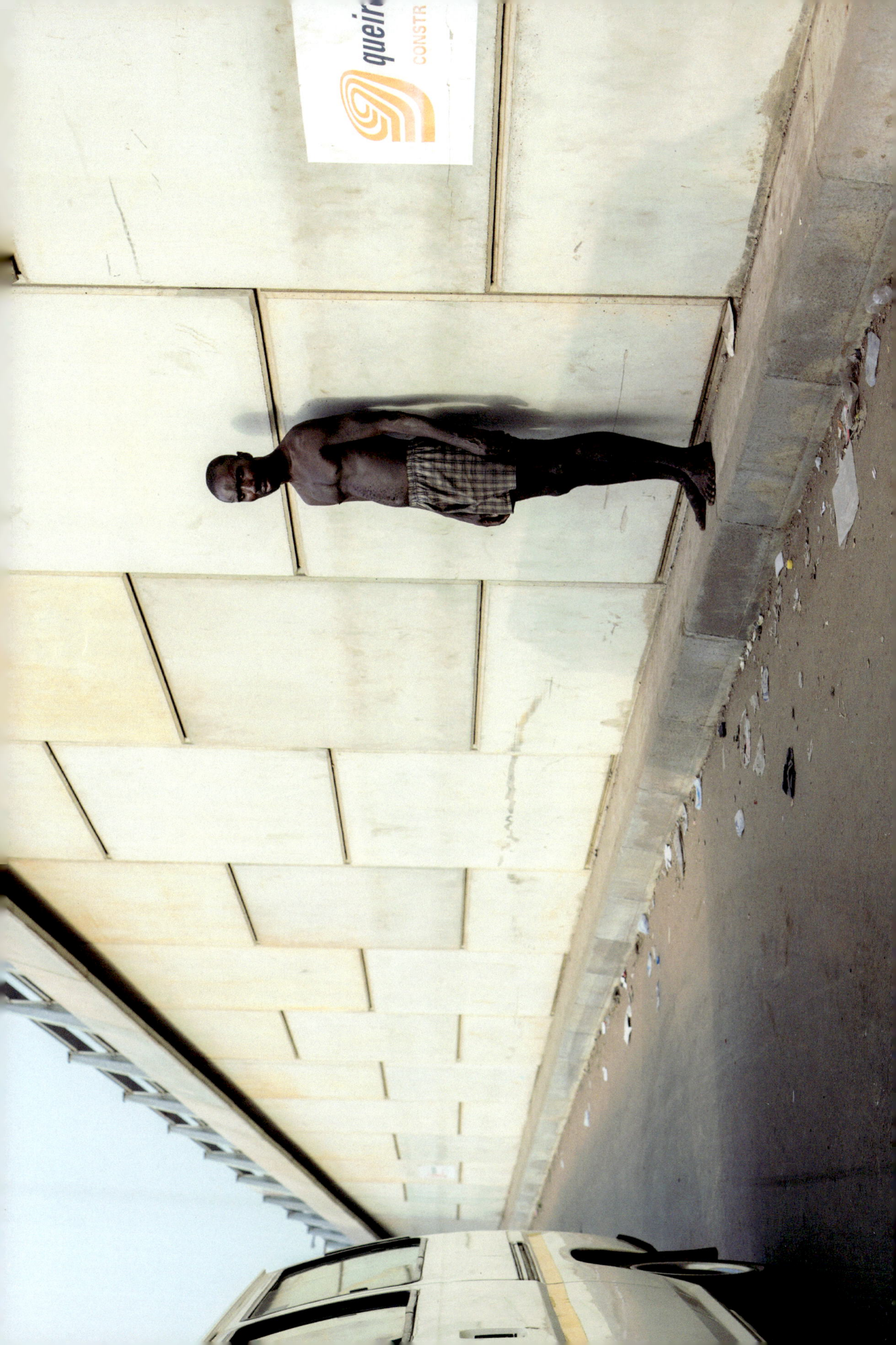

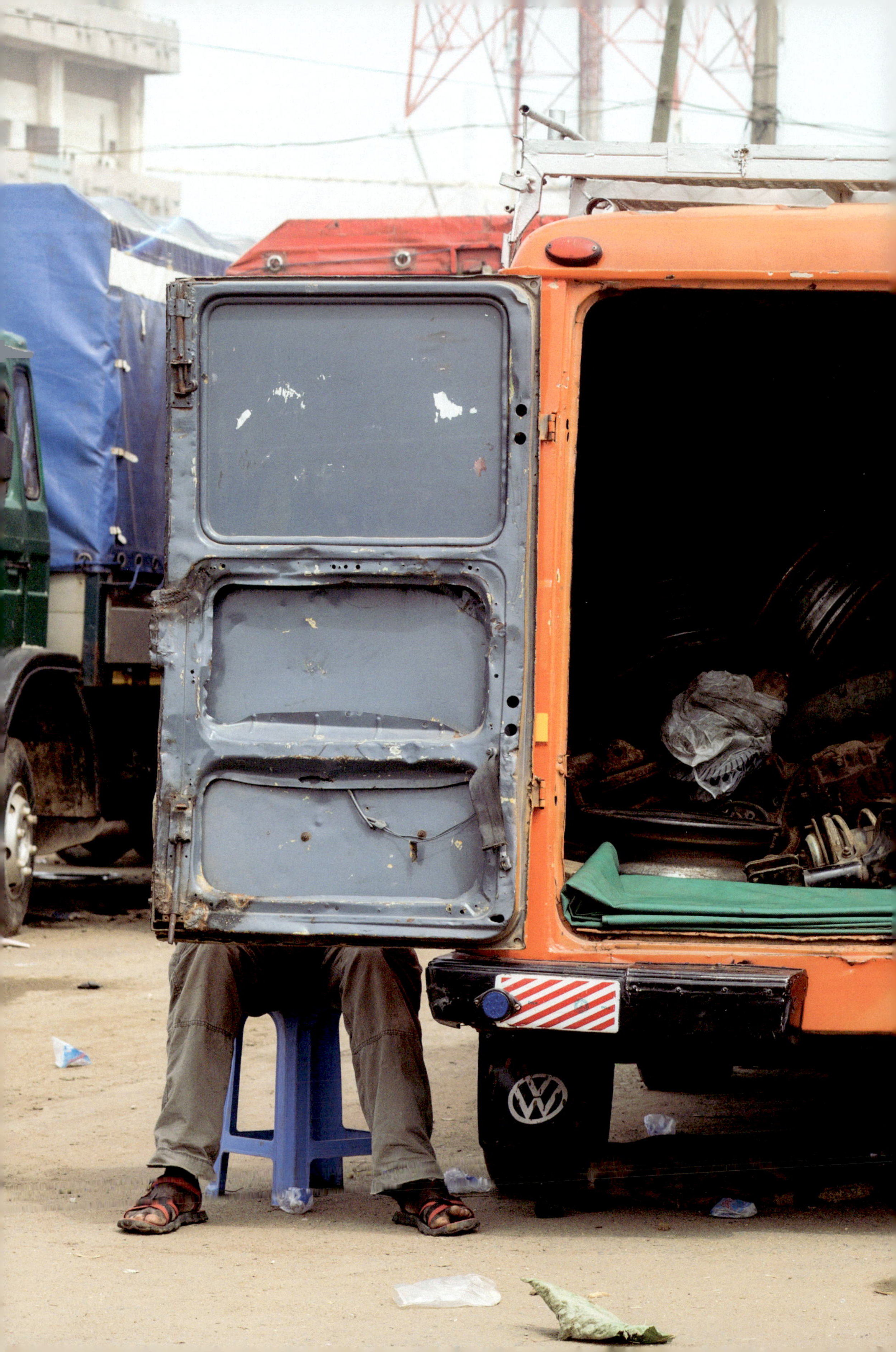

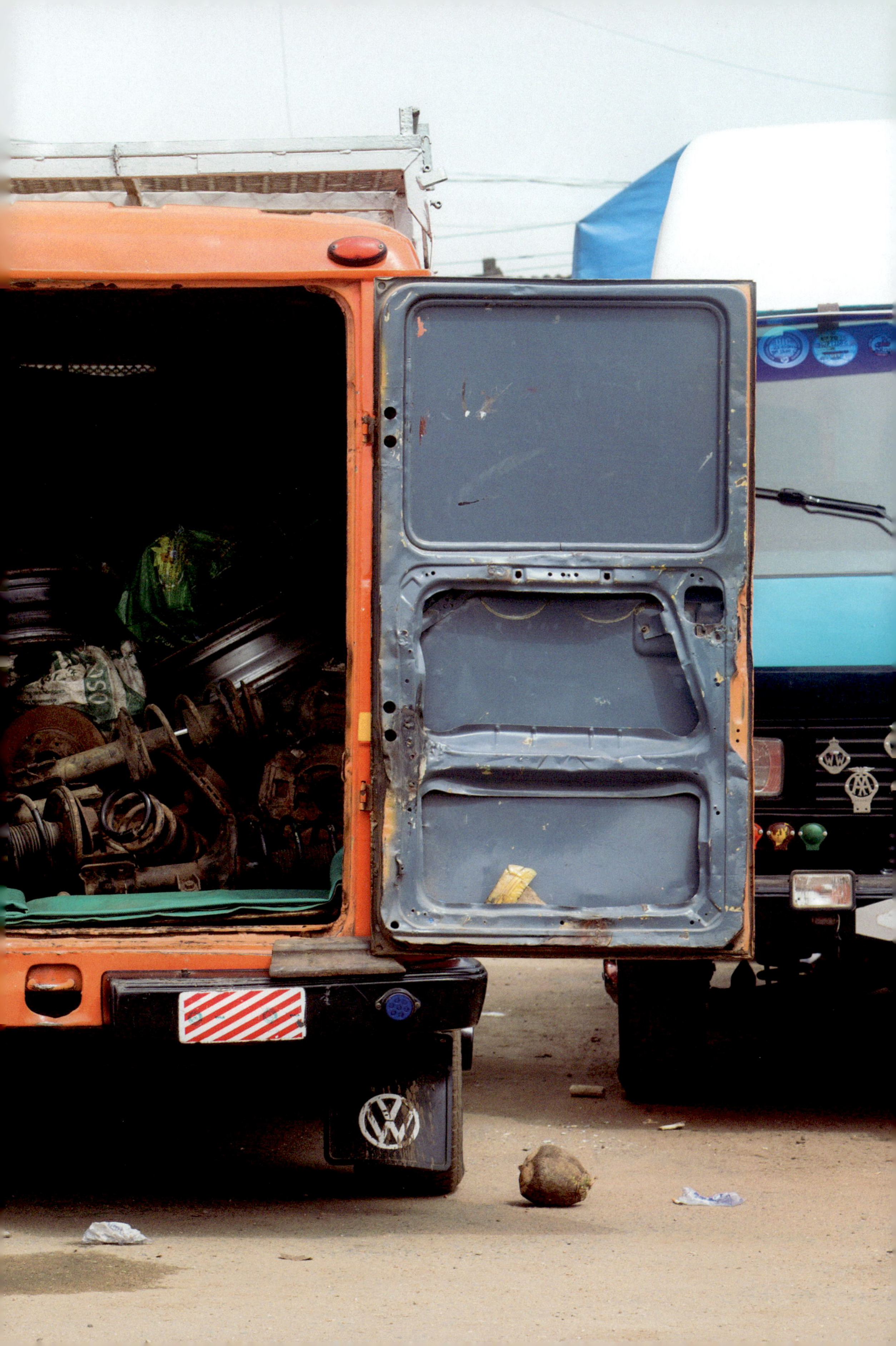

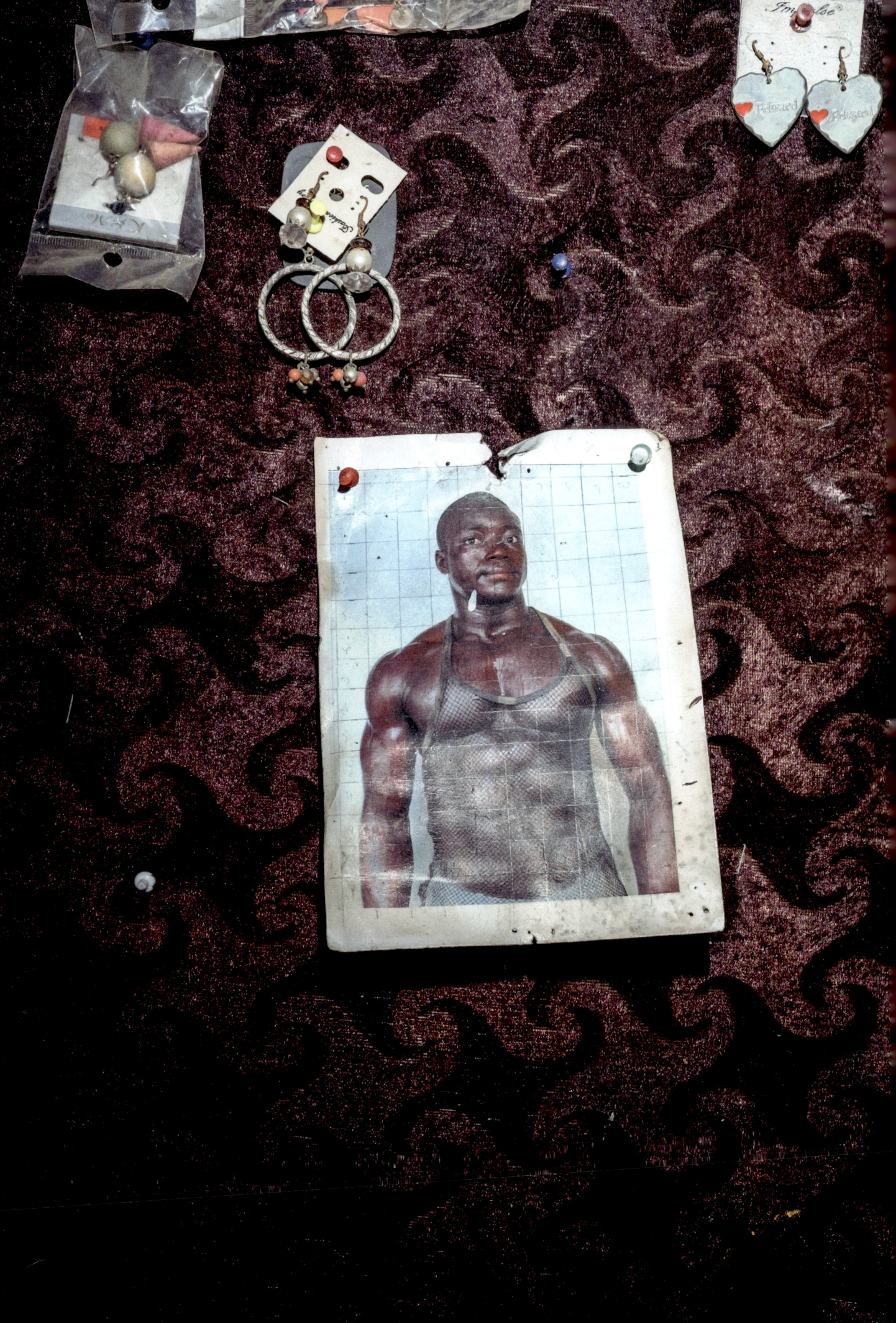

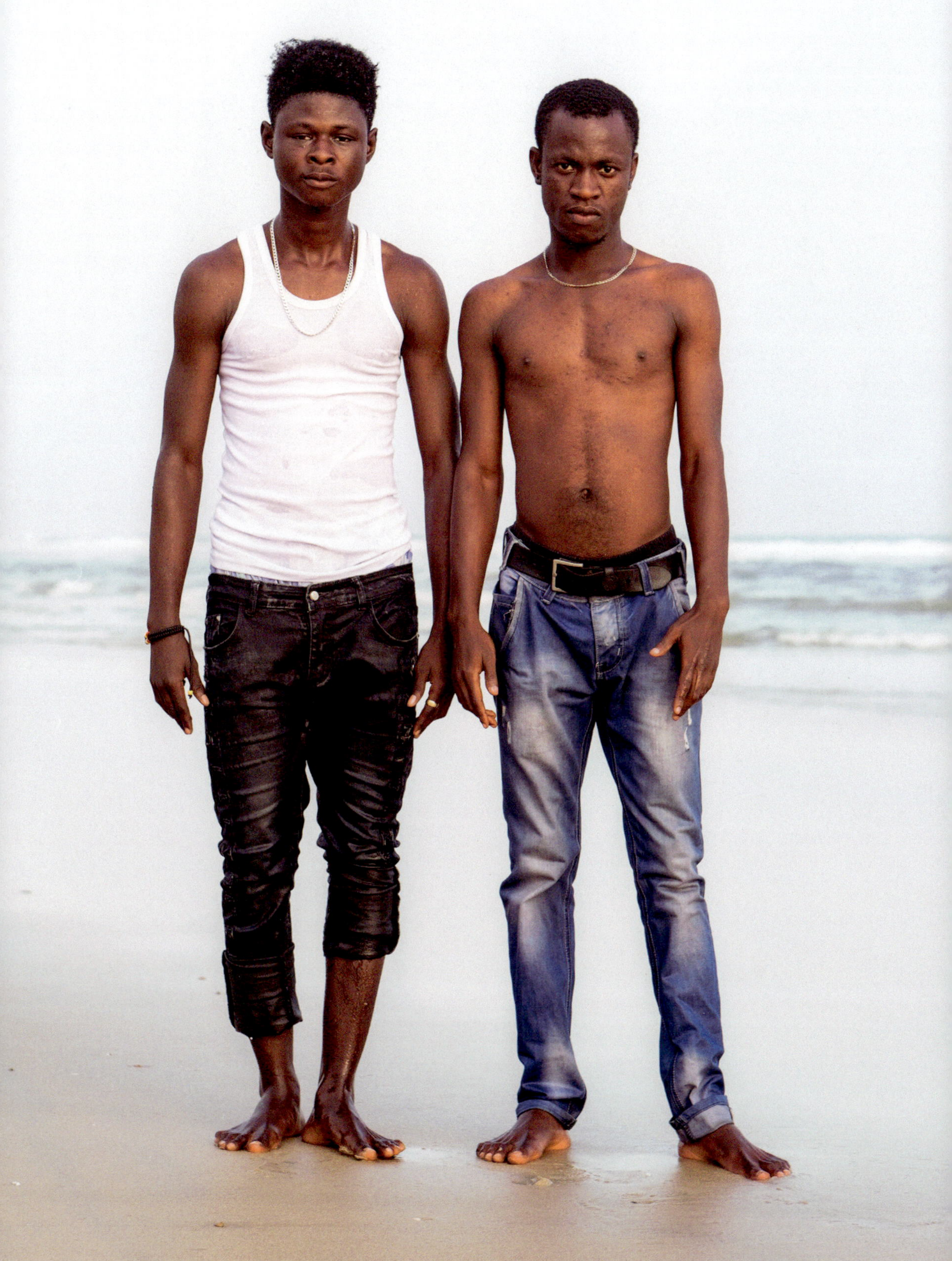

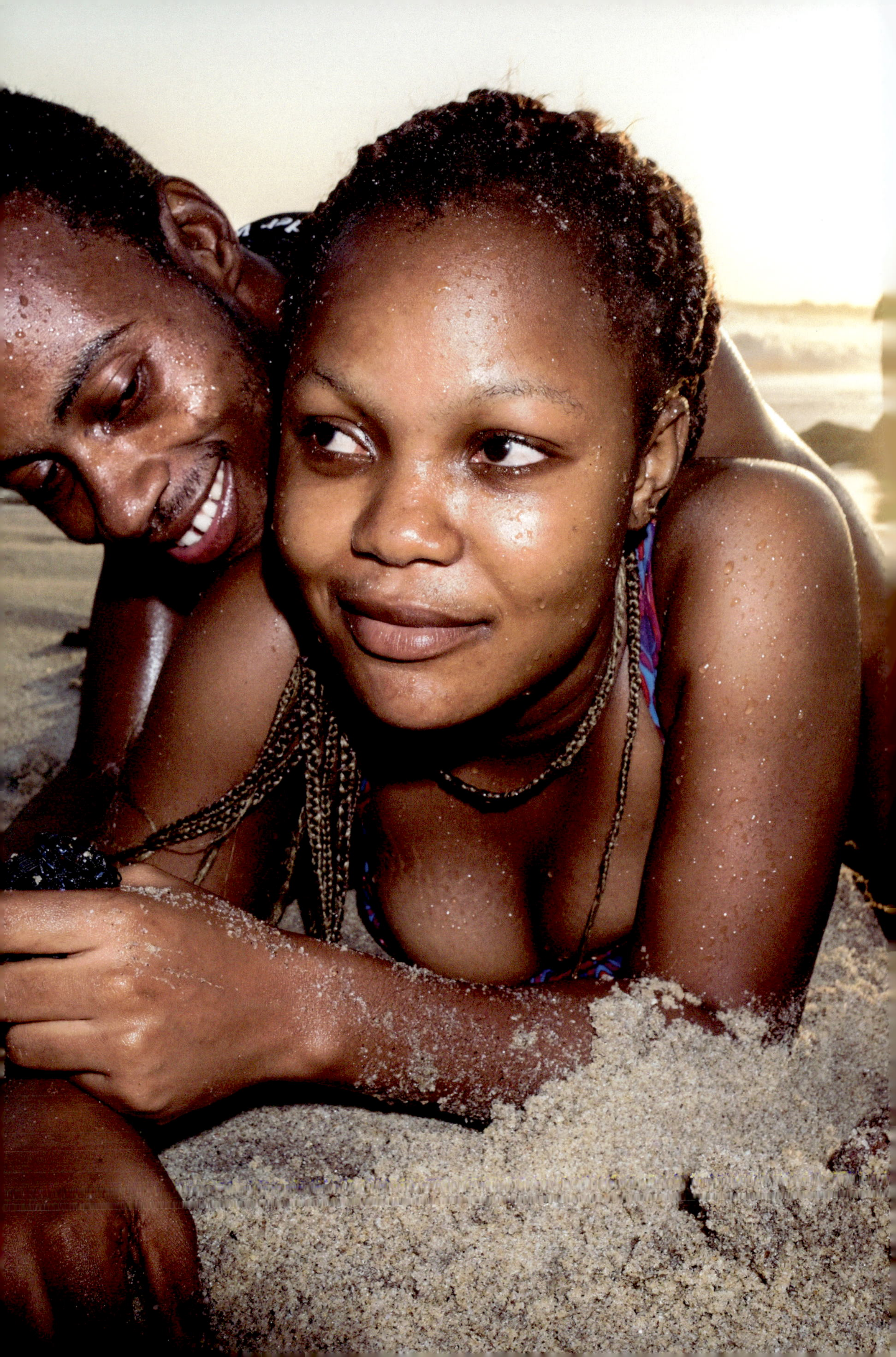

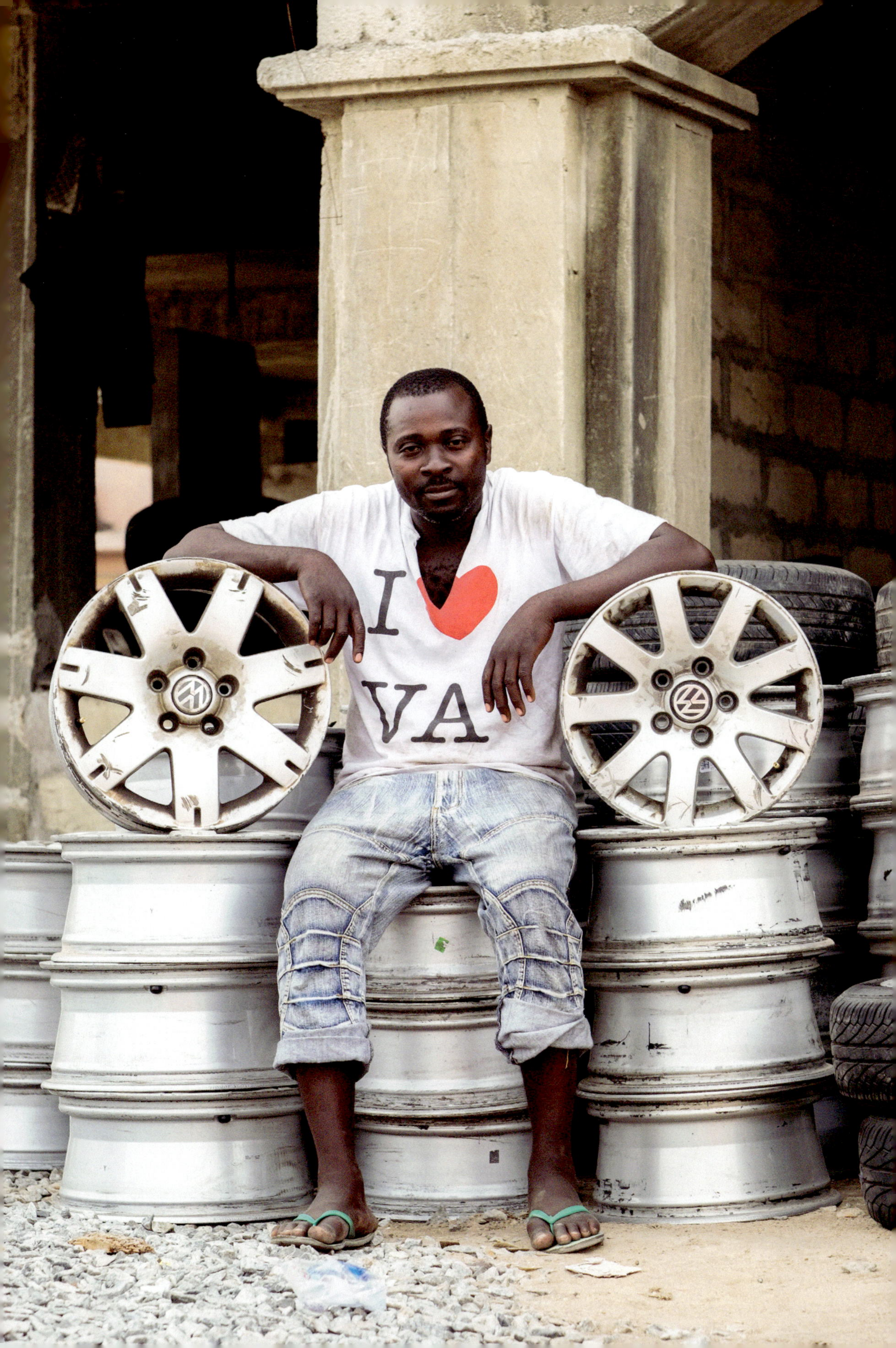
I ♥
VA

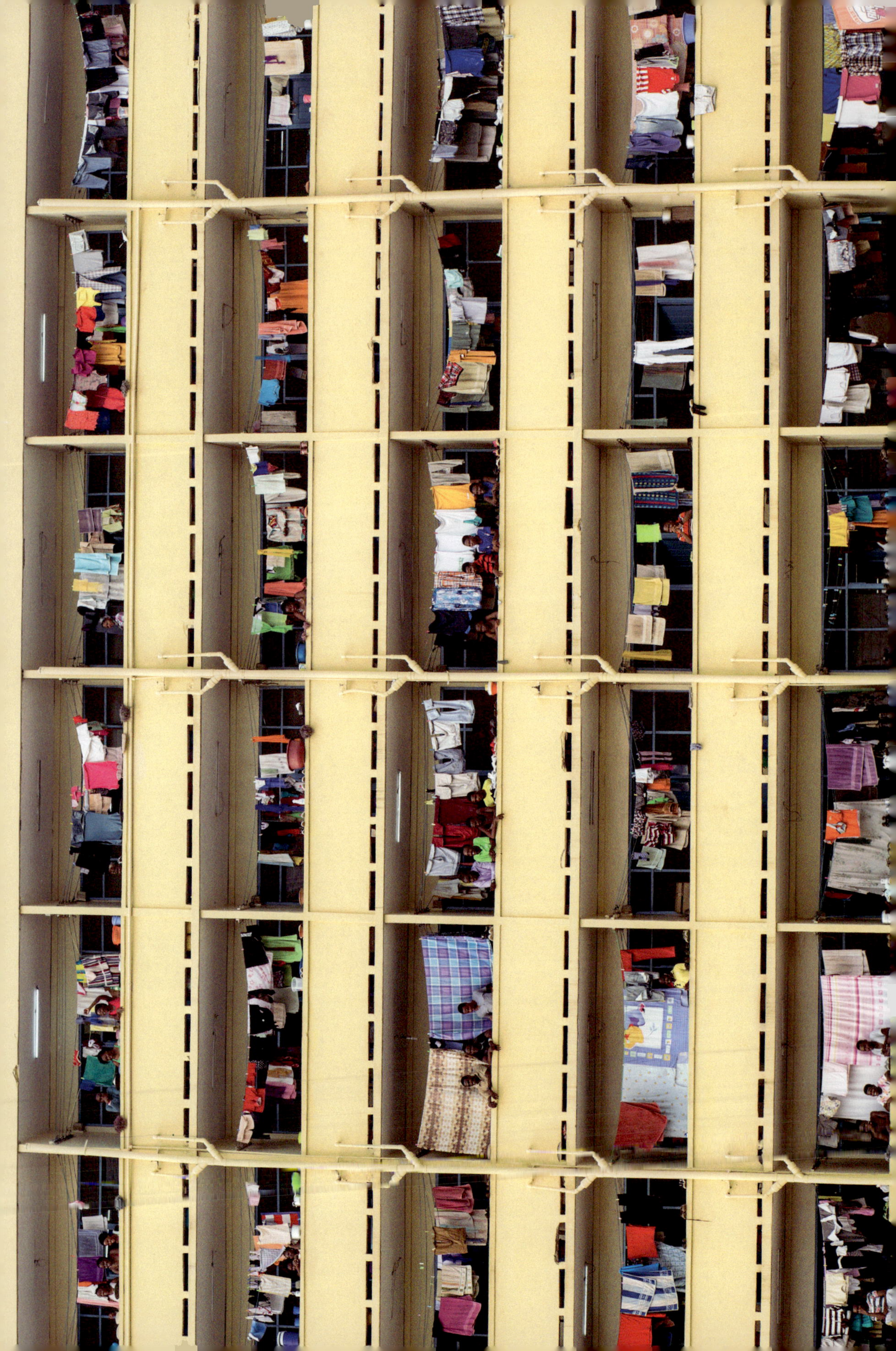

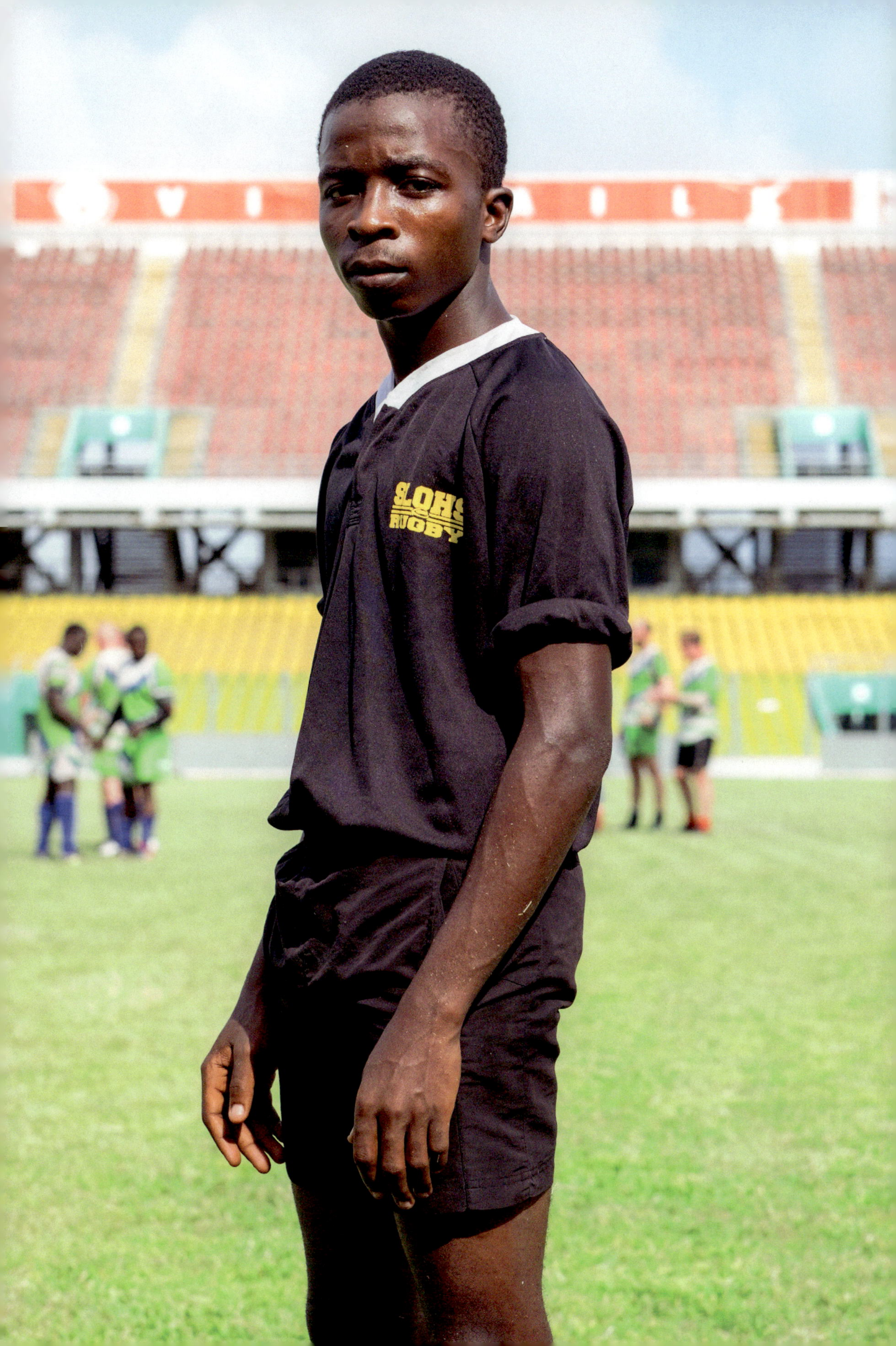
SLOHS
RUGBY

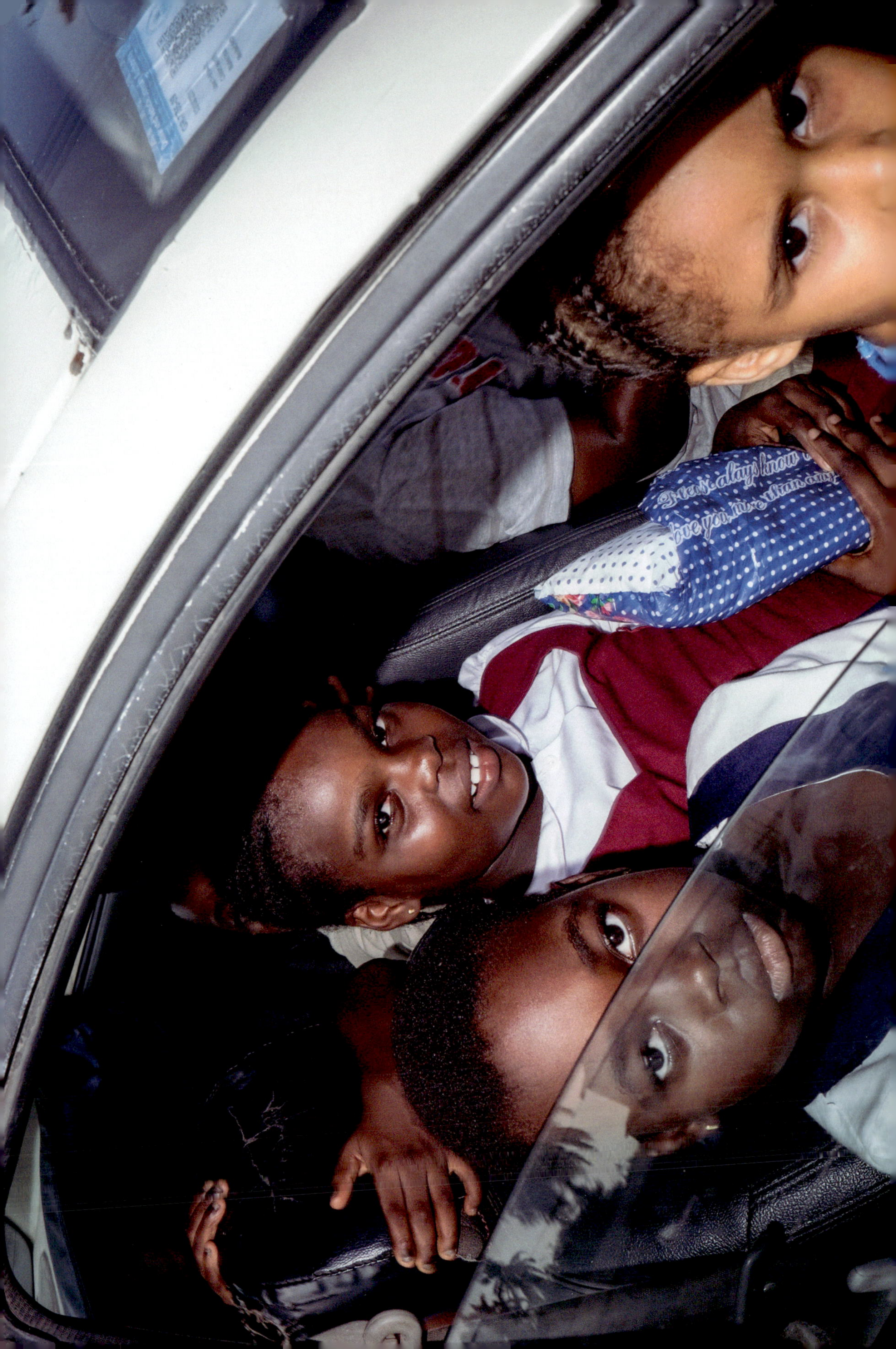

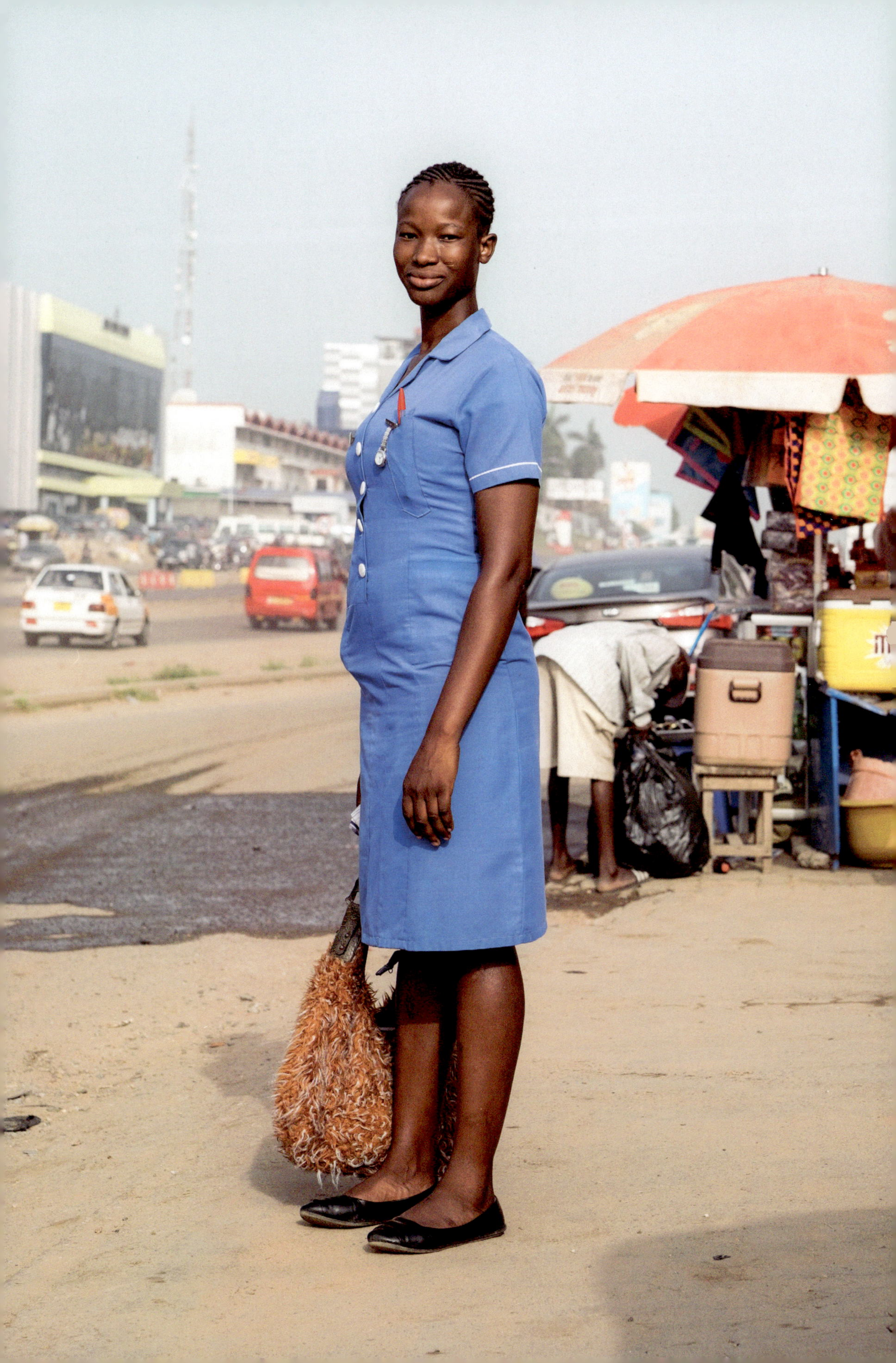

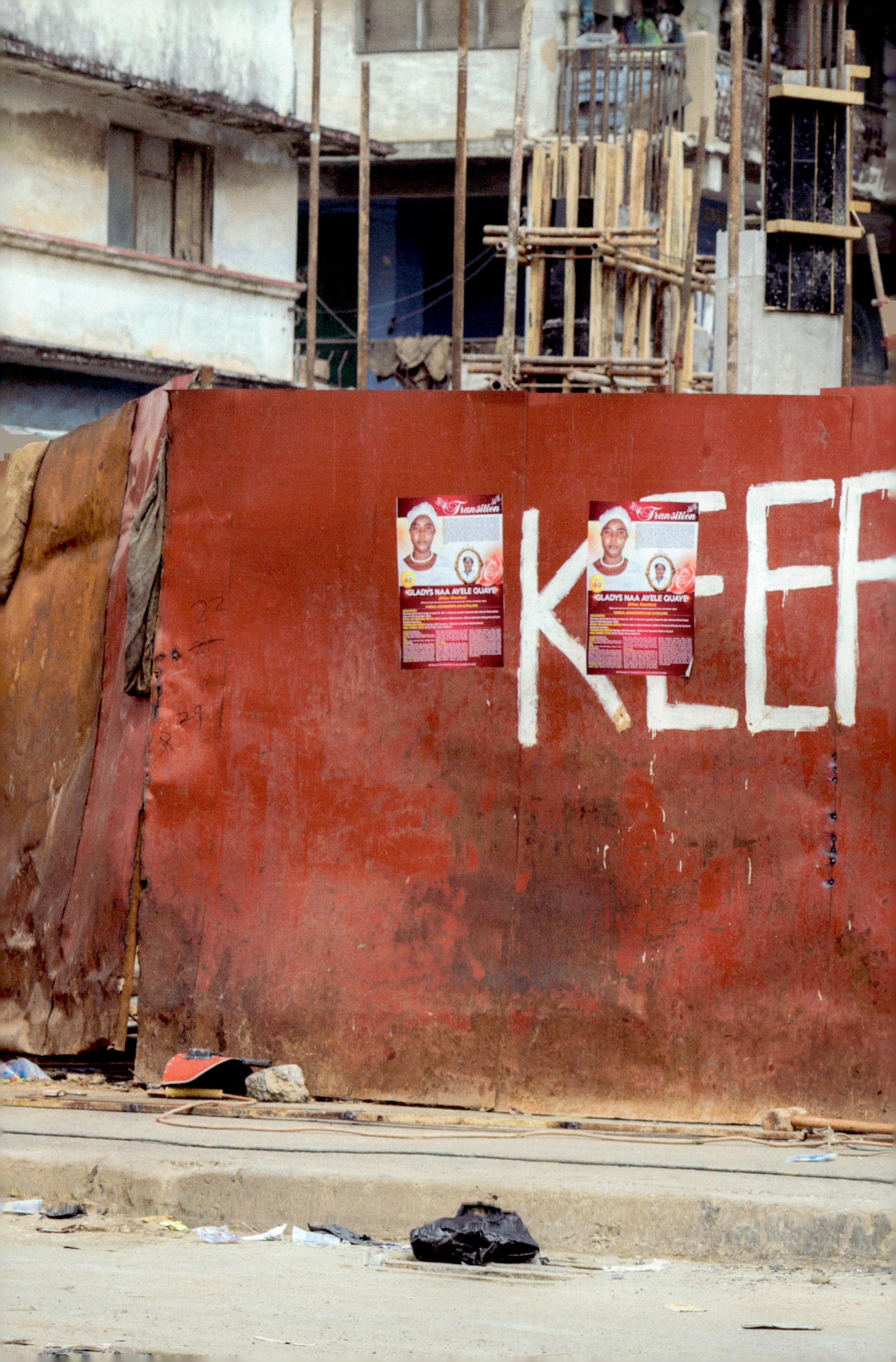
Transition
GLADYS NAA AYELE QUAYE
KEE

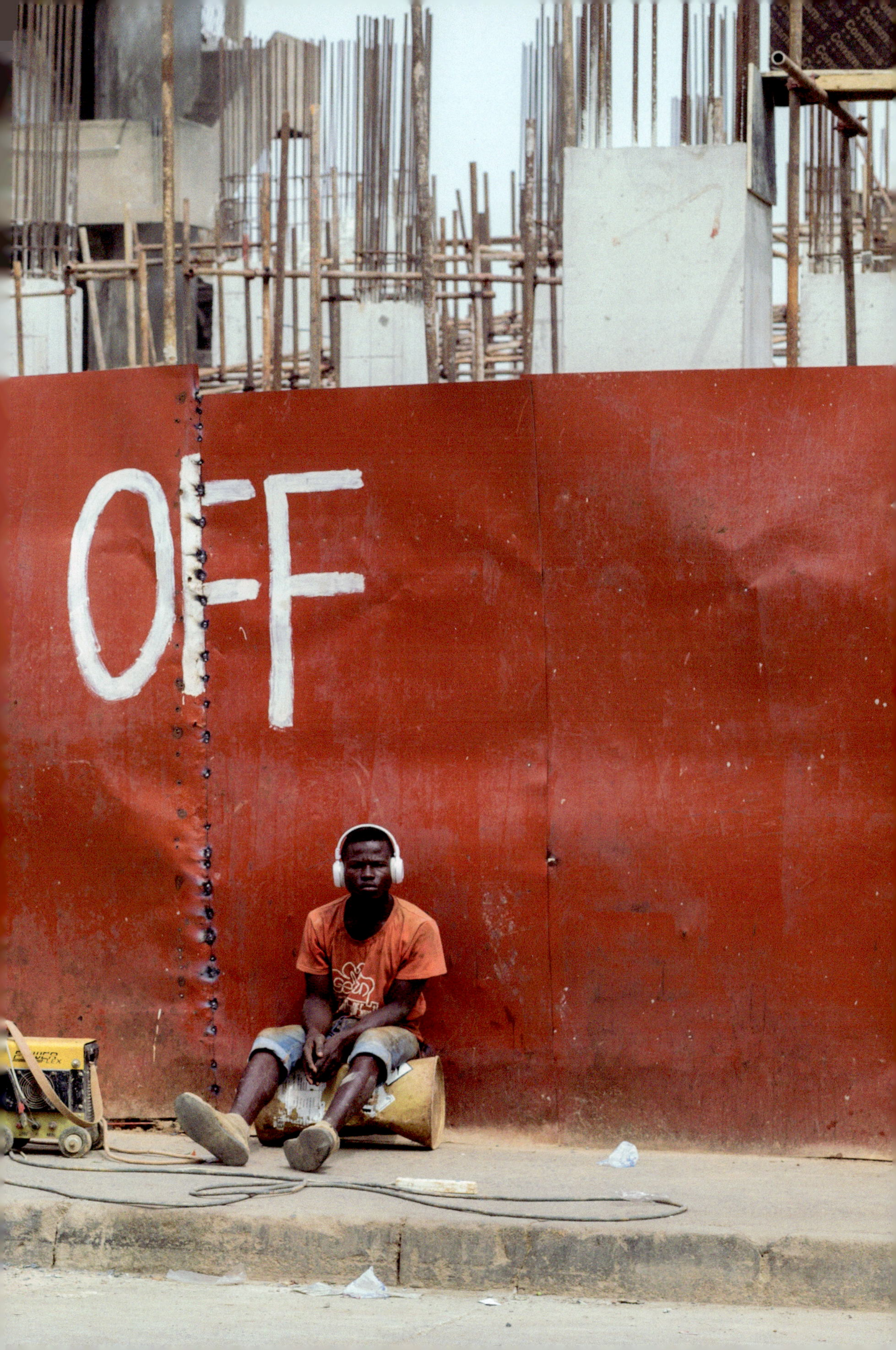
OFF

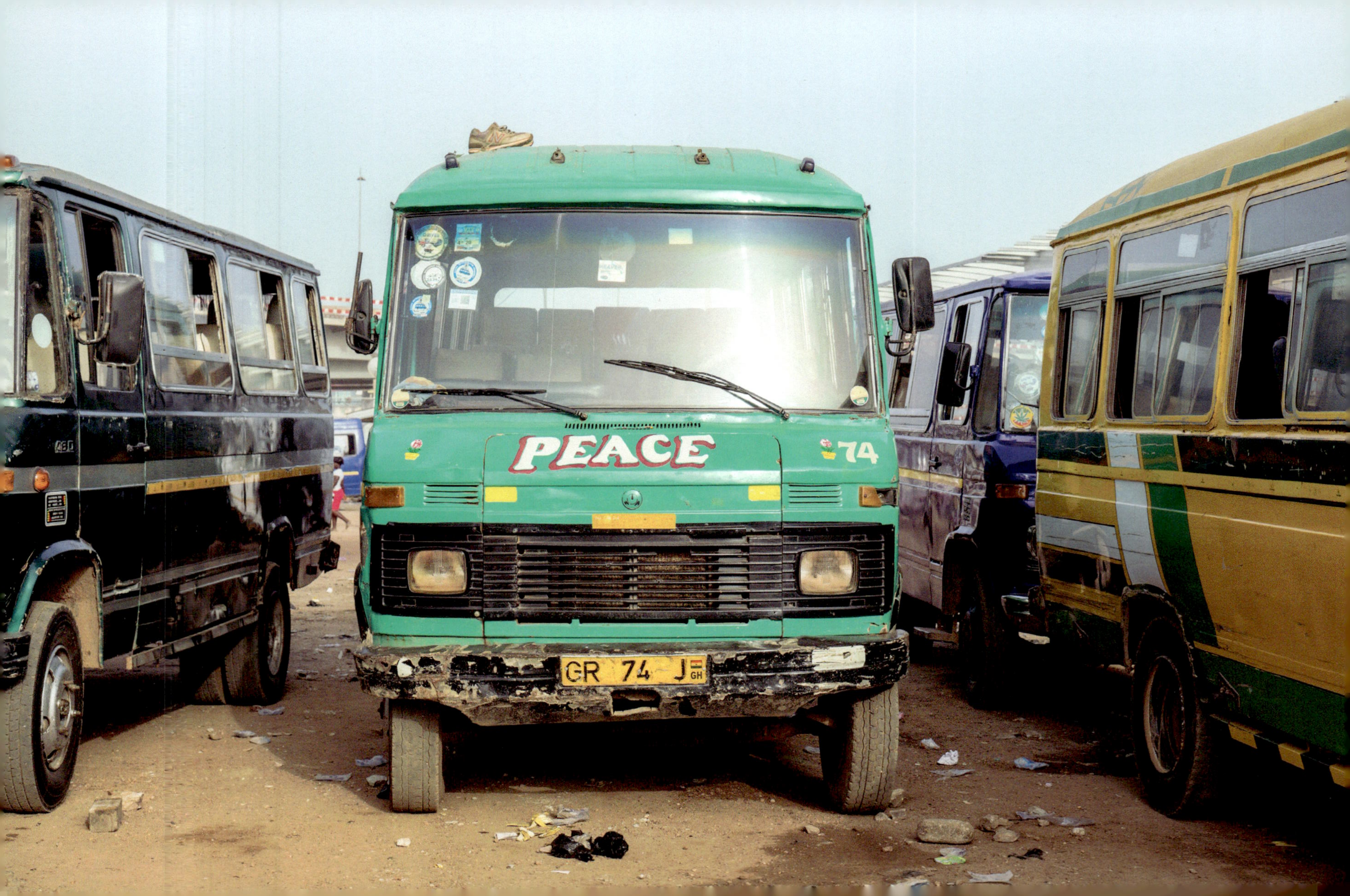
PEACE
74
GR 74 J GH

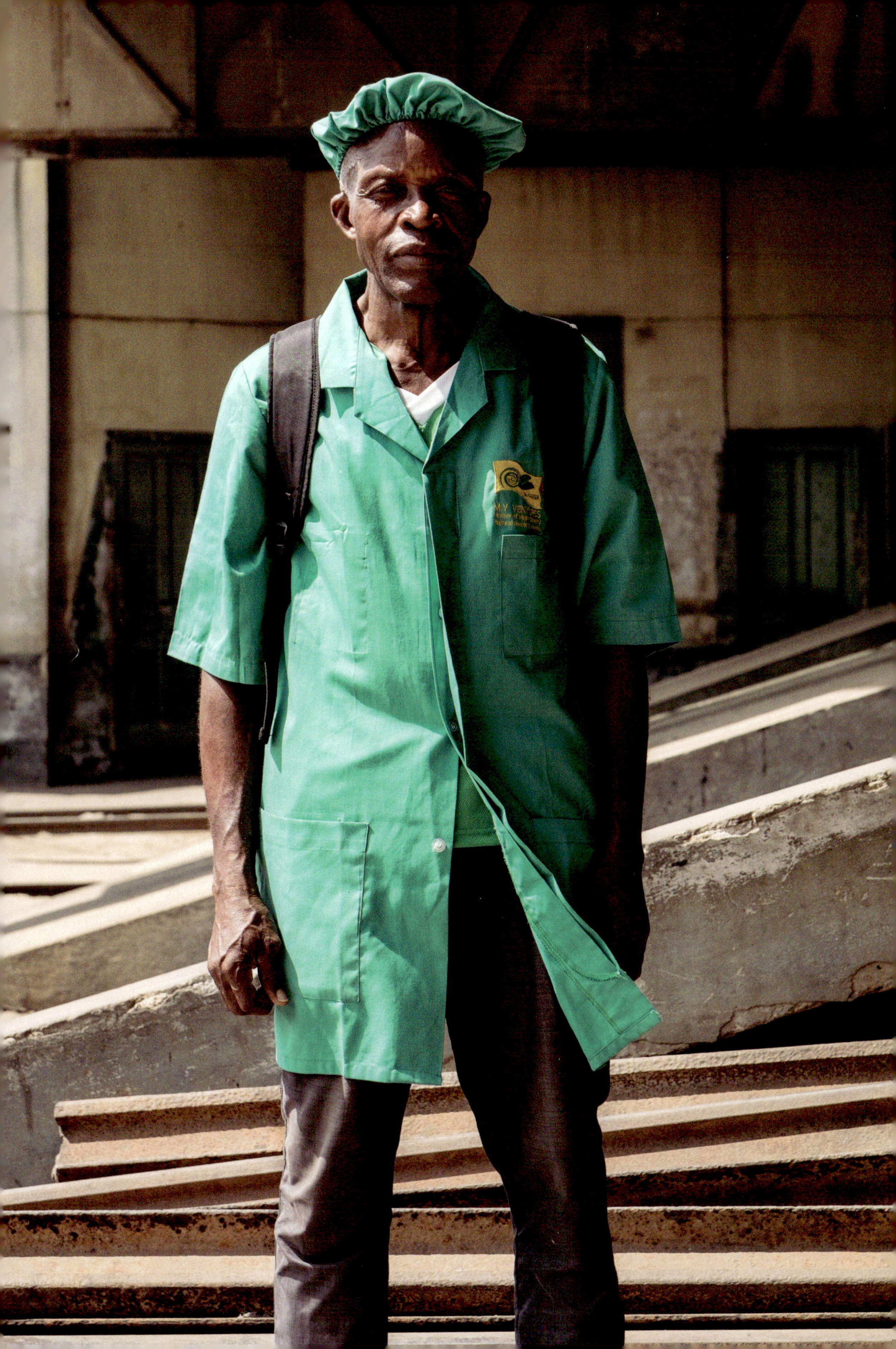

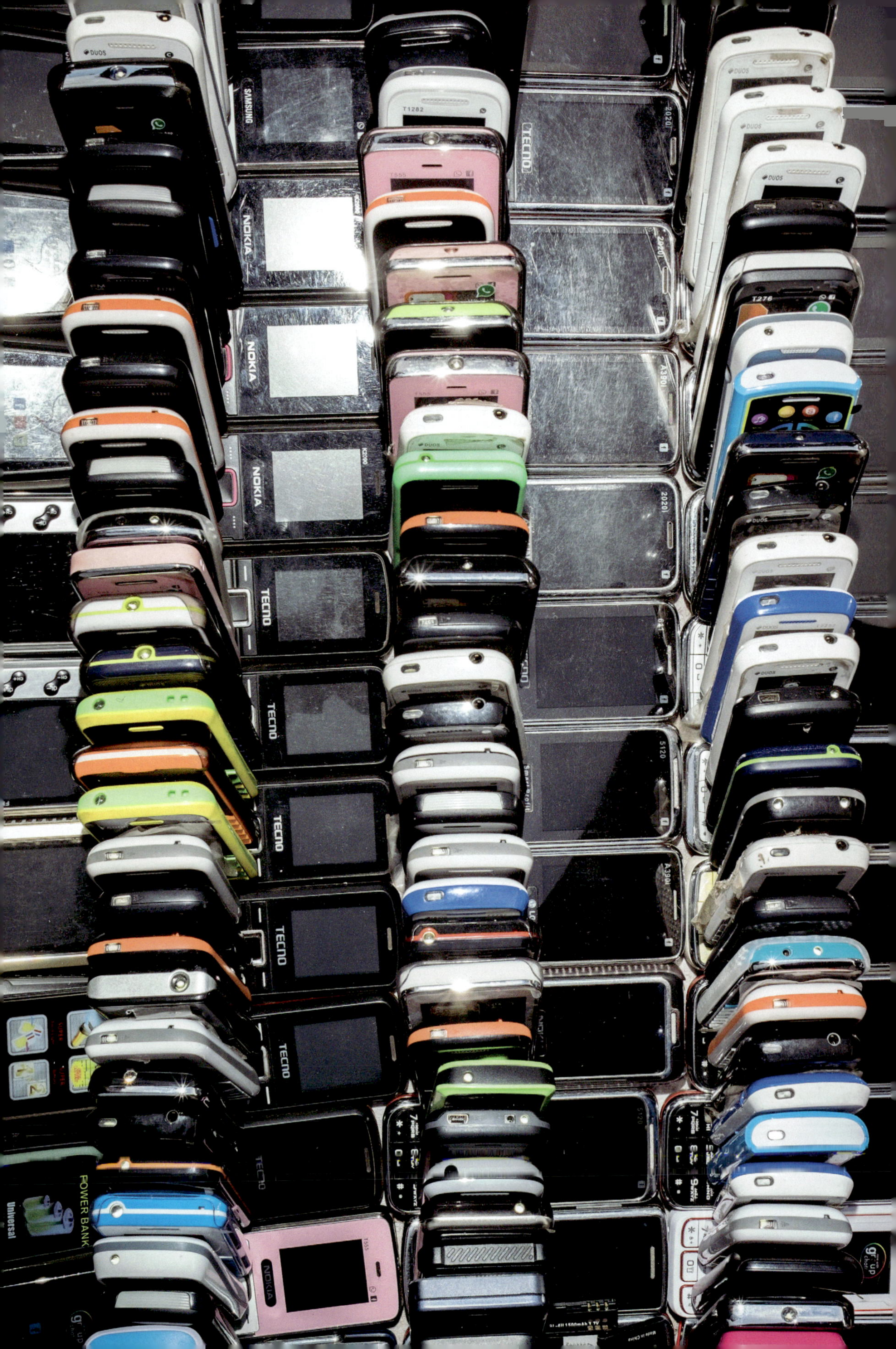
SAMSUNG
NOKIA
NOKIA
NOKIA
TECNO
TECNO
TECNO
TECNO
TECNO
TECNO
TECNO
POWER BANK
Universal

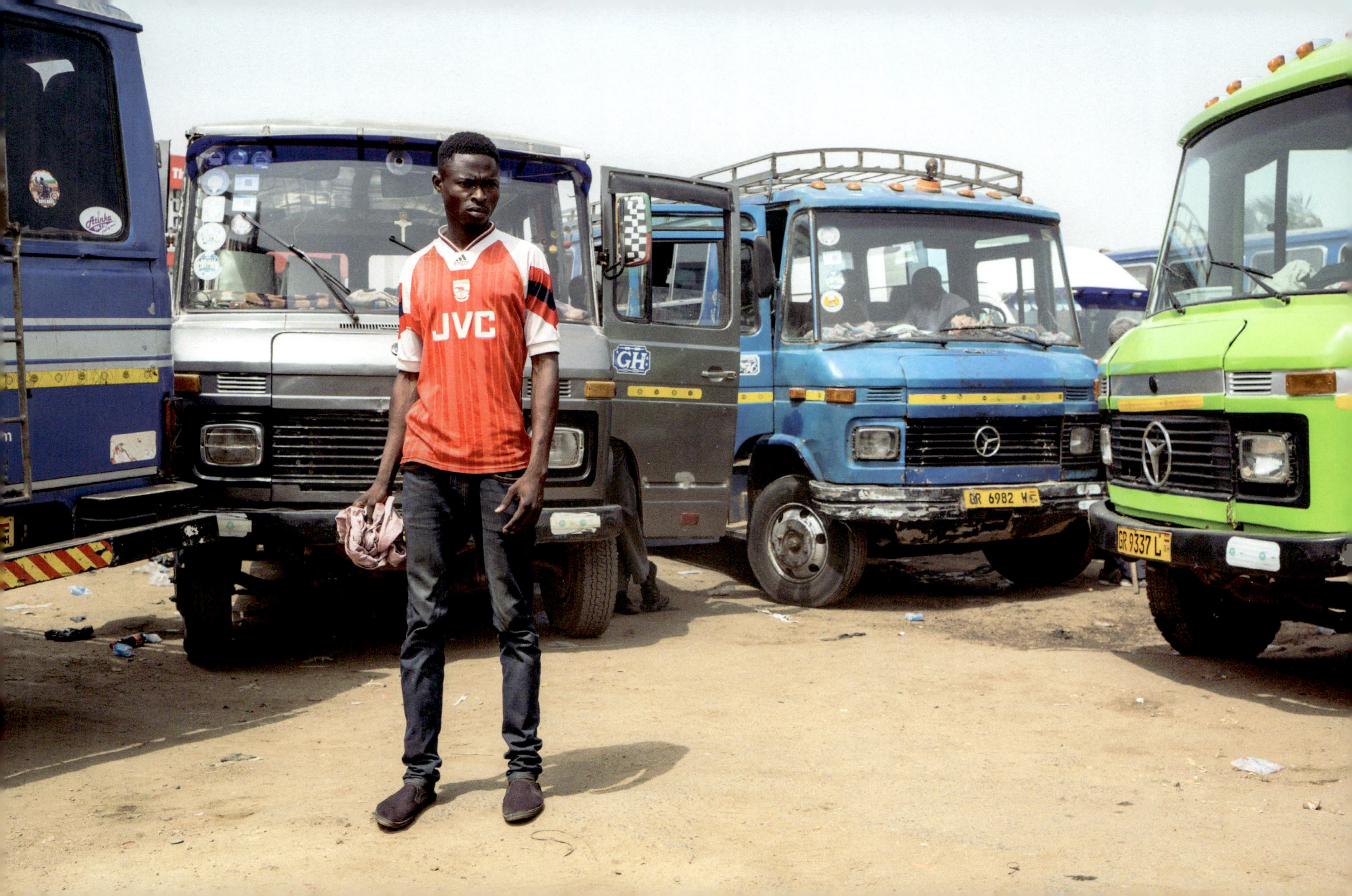
Atinka
JVC
GH
GR 6982 H
GR 9337 L

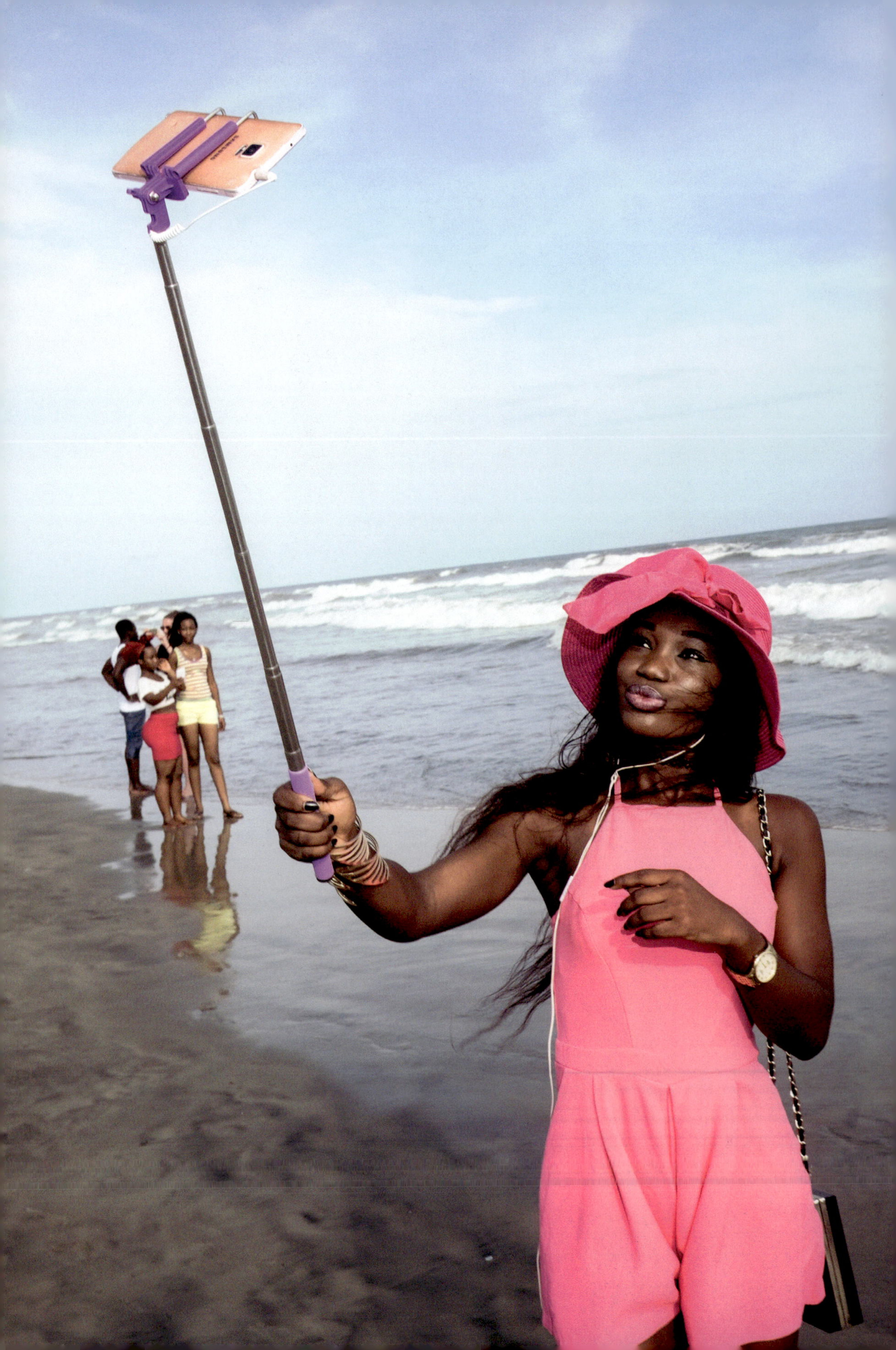

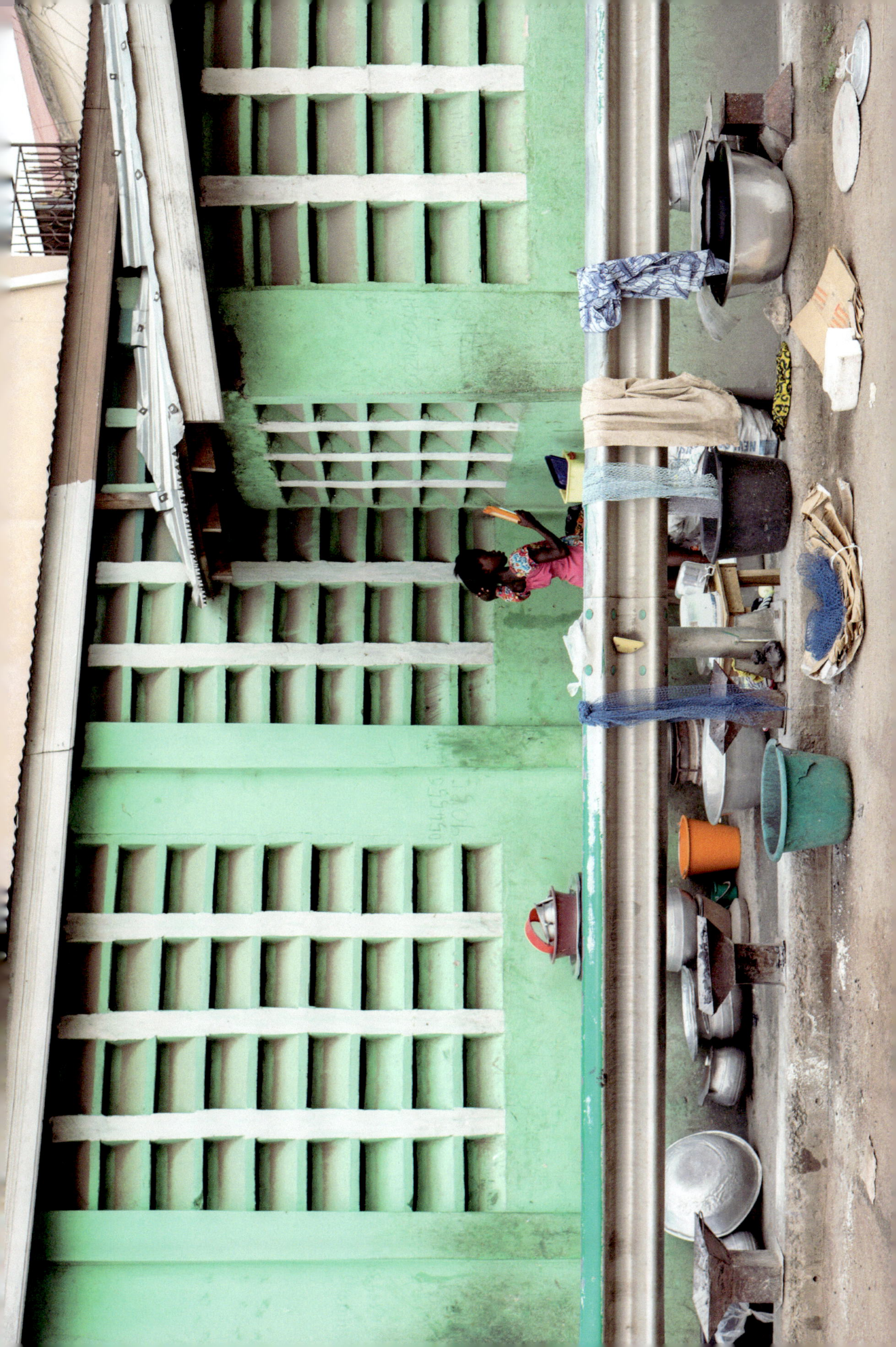

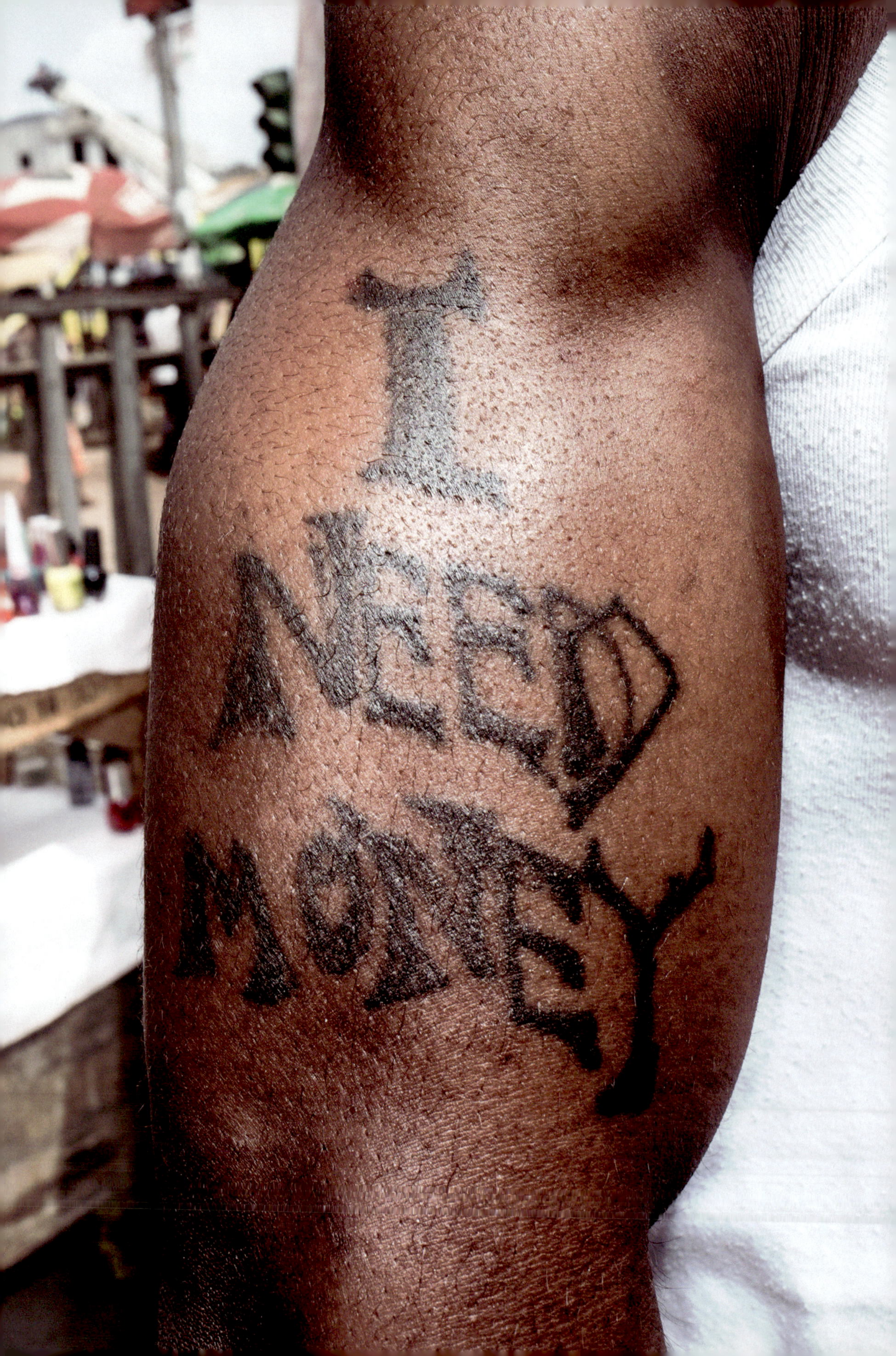
I
NEED
MONEY

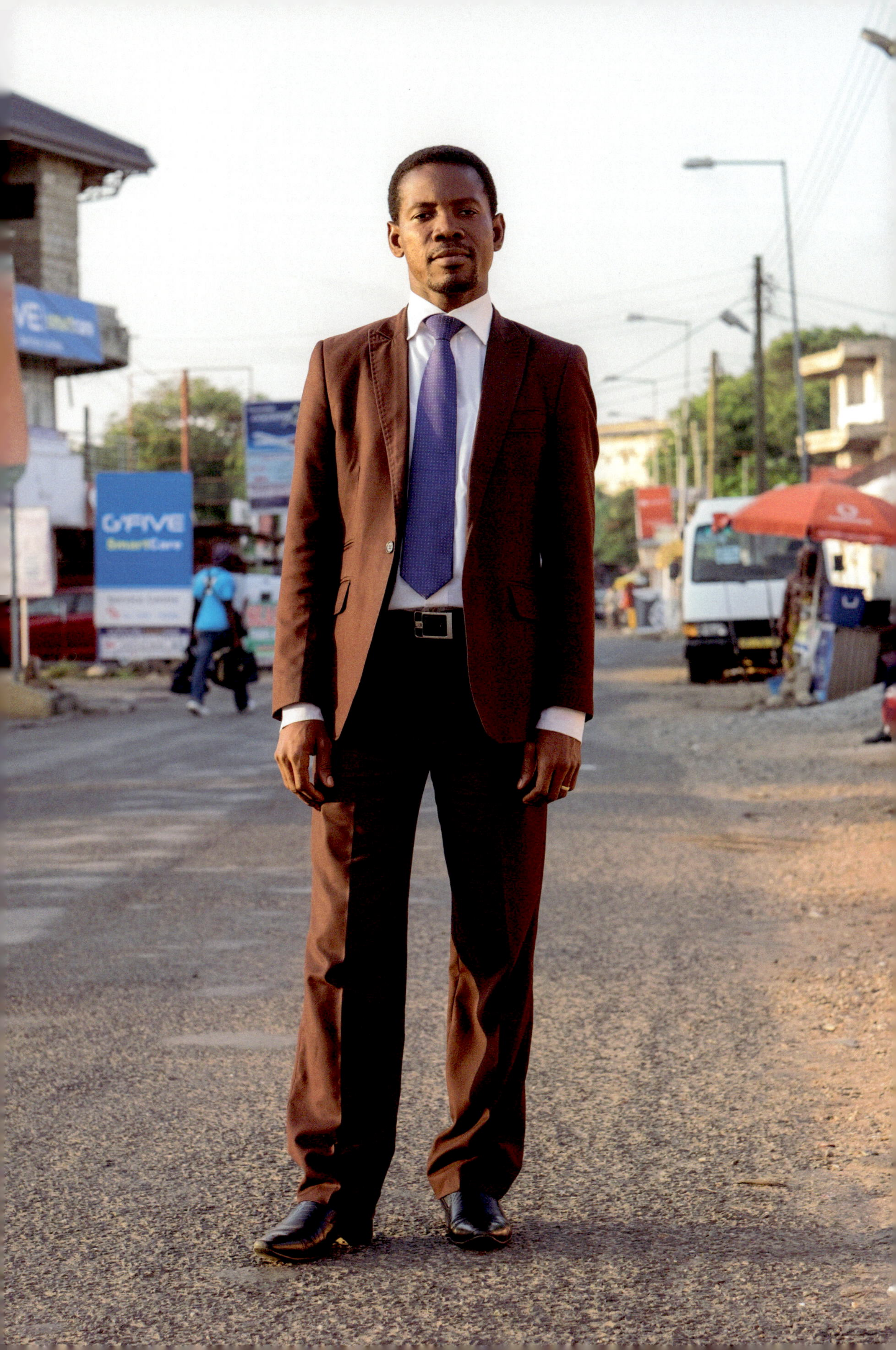
G'FIVE

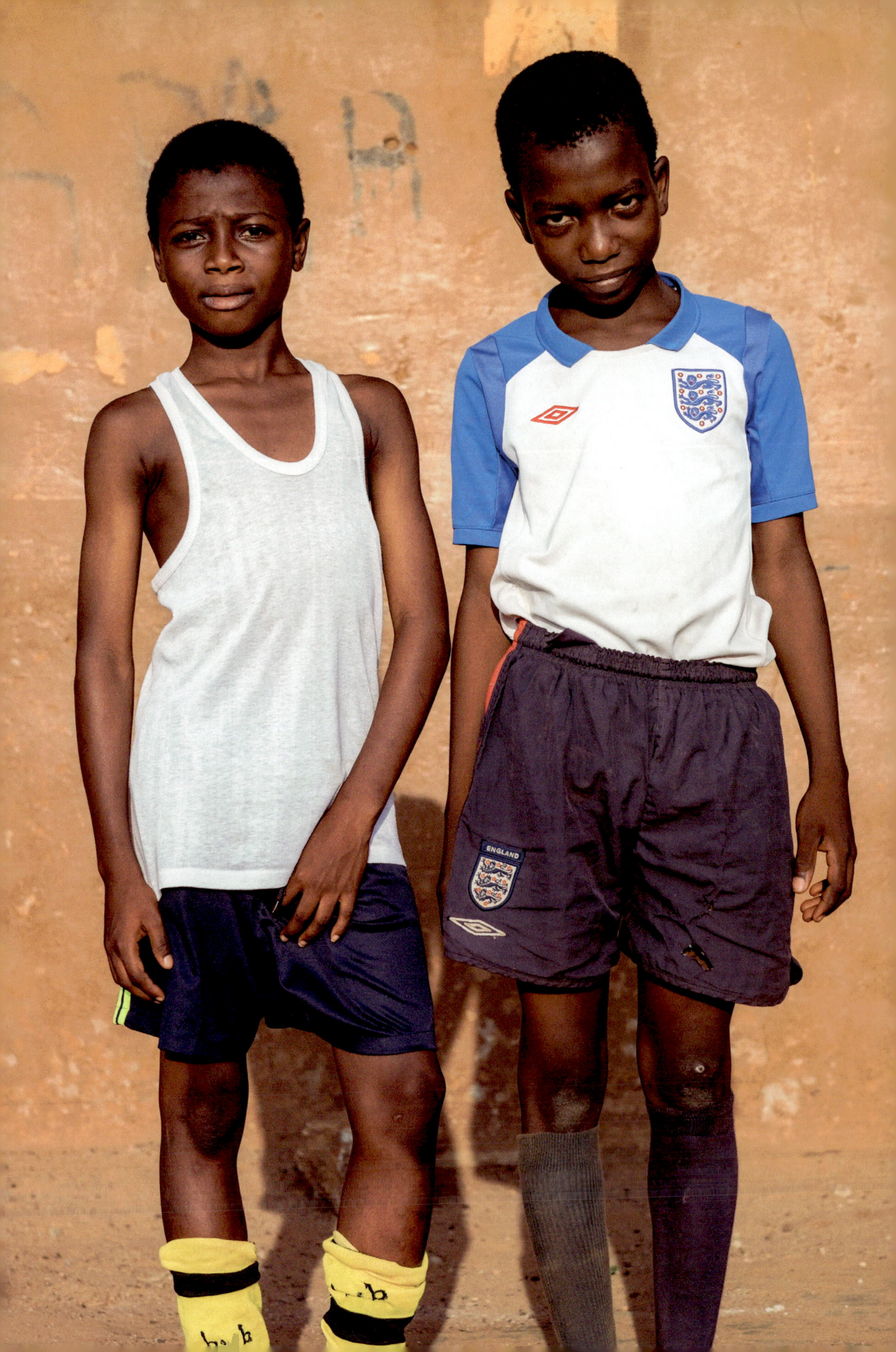
ENGLAND

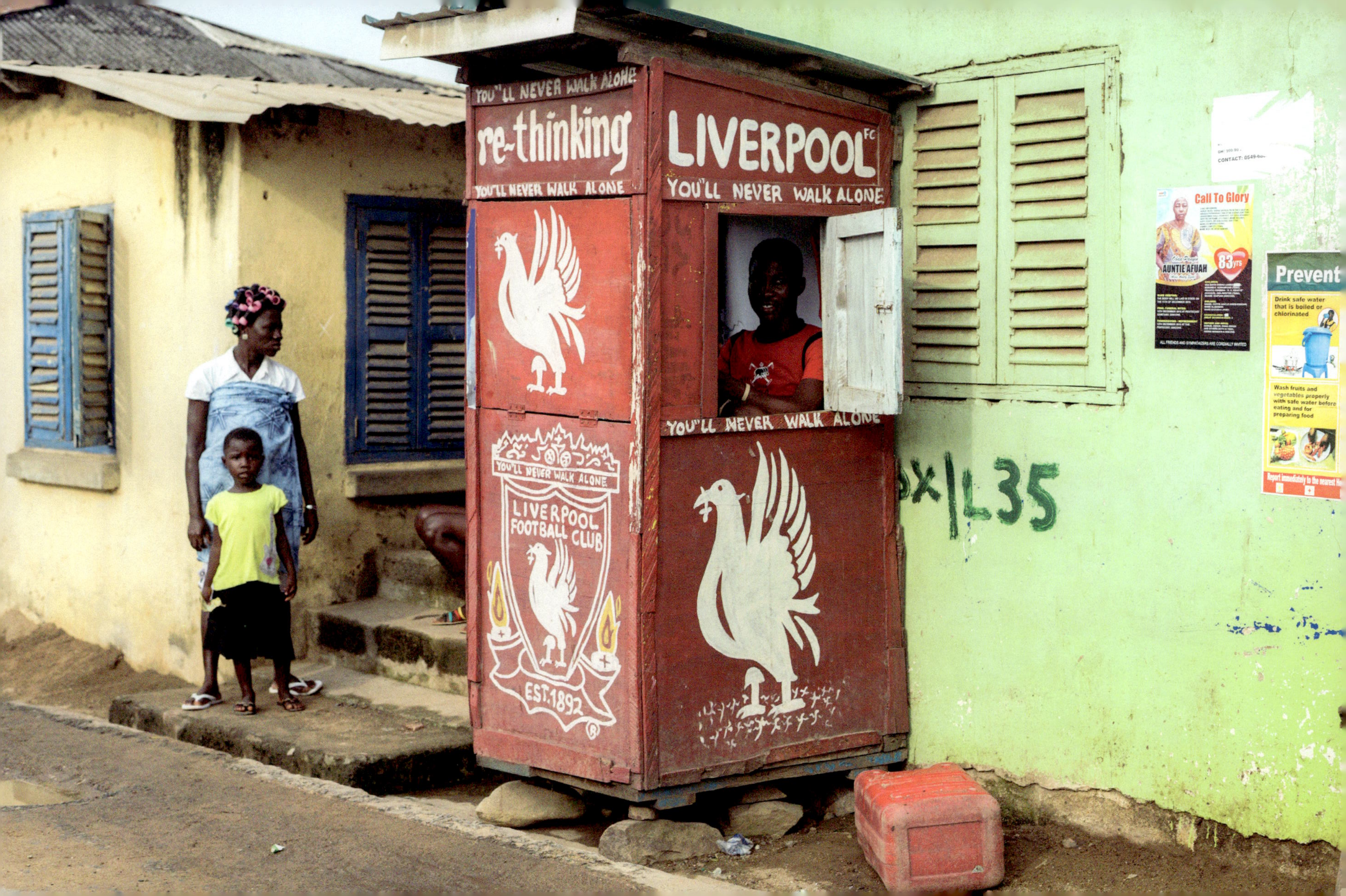

YOU'LL NEVER WALK ALONE
re-thinking
YOU'LL NEVER WALK ALONE
LIVERPOOL FC
YOU'LL NEVER WALK ALONE
YOU'LL NEVER WALK ALONE
YOU'LL NEVER WALK ALONE
LIVERPOOL FOOTBALL CLUB
EST. 1892
X|L35
Call To Glory
AUNTIE AFUAH
83yrs
Prevent
Drink safe water that is boiled or chlorinated
Wash fruits and vegetables properly with safe water before eating and for preparing food

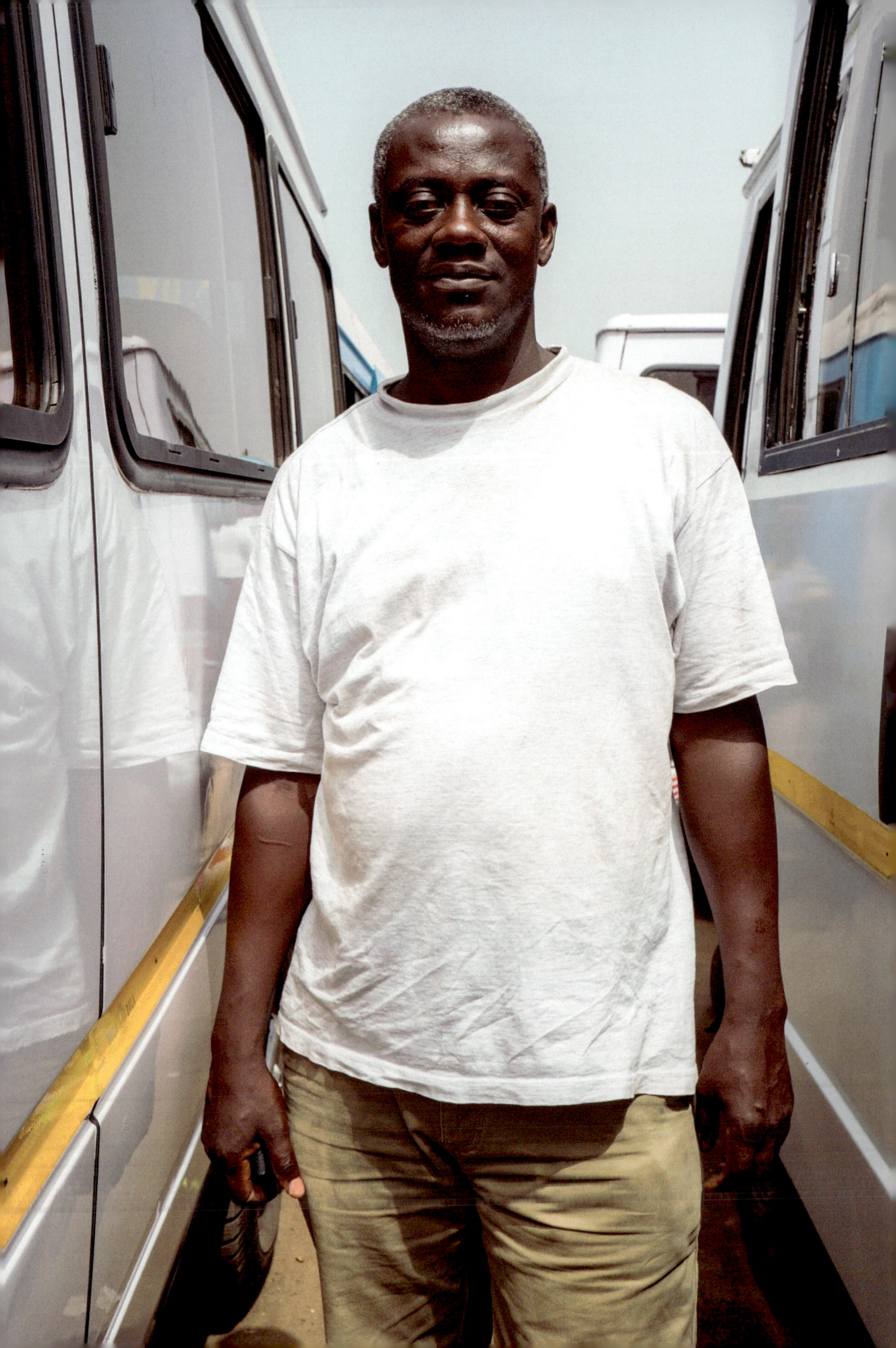

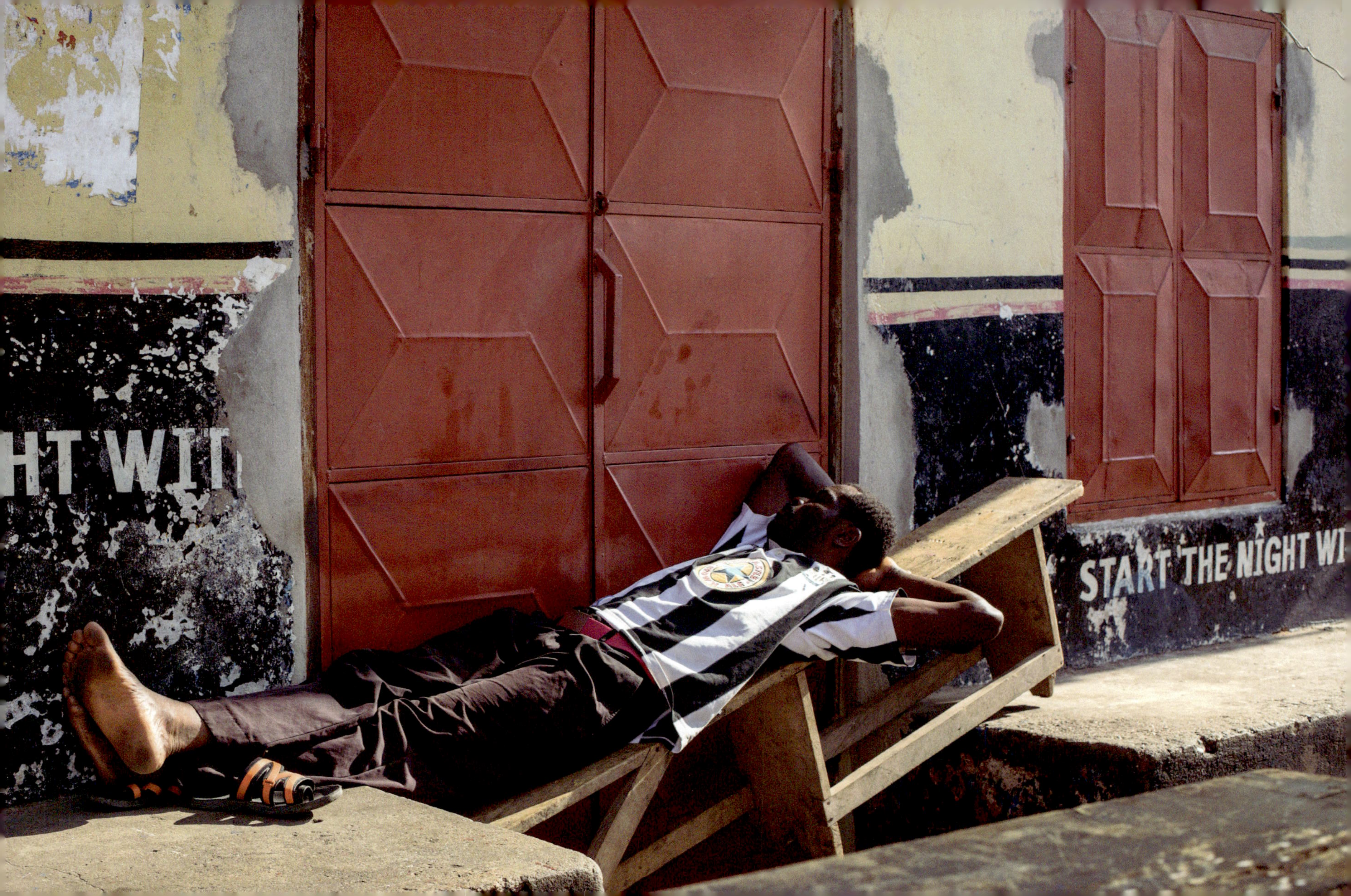
HT WI
START THE NIGHT WI

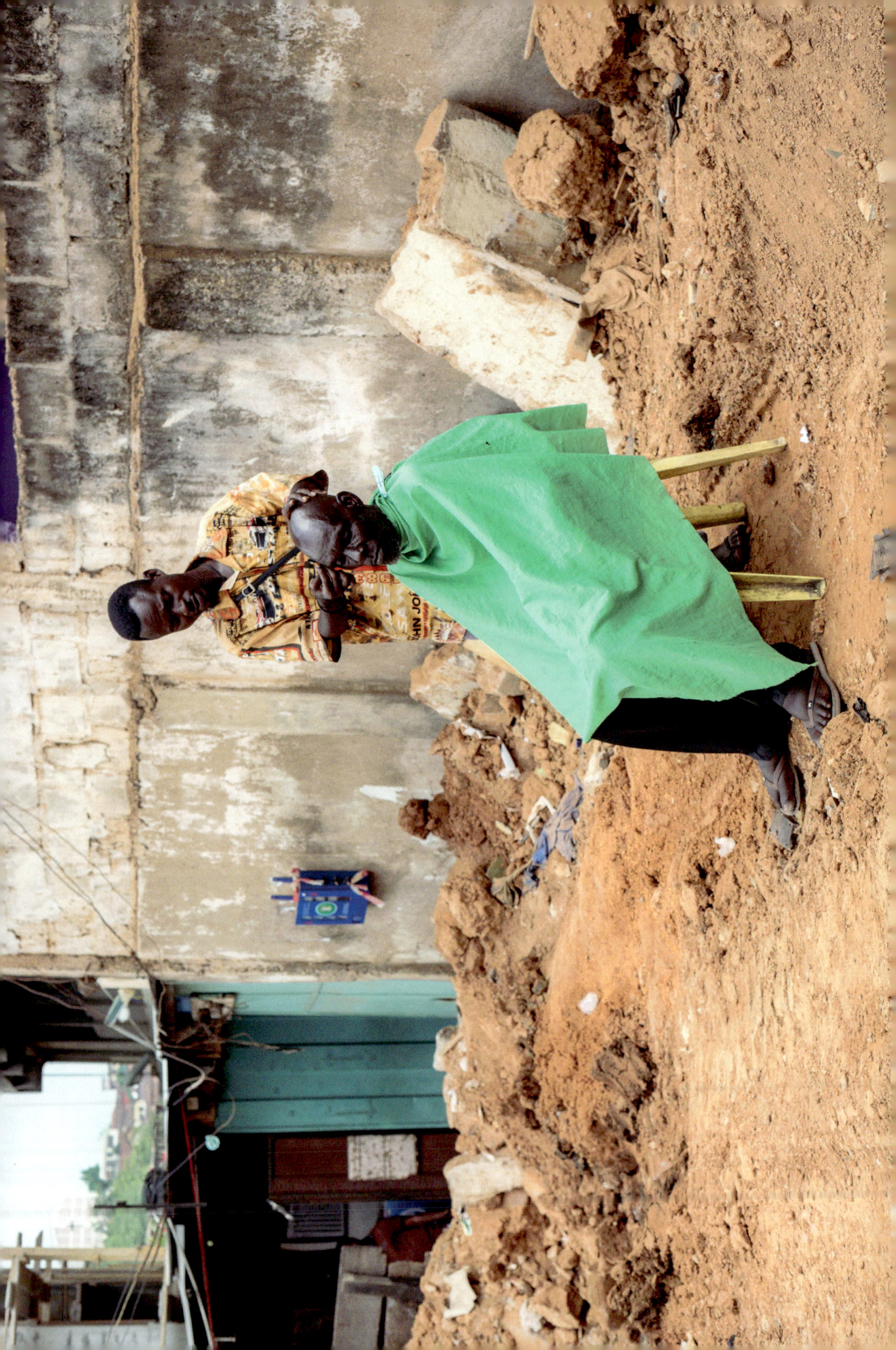

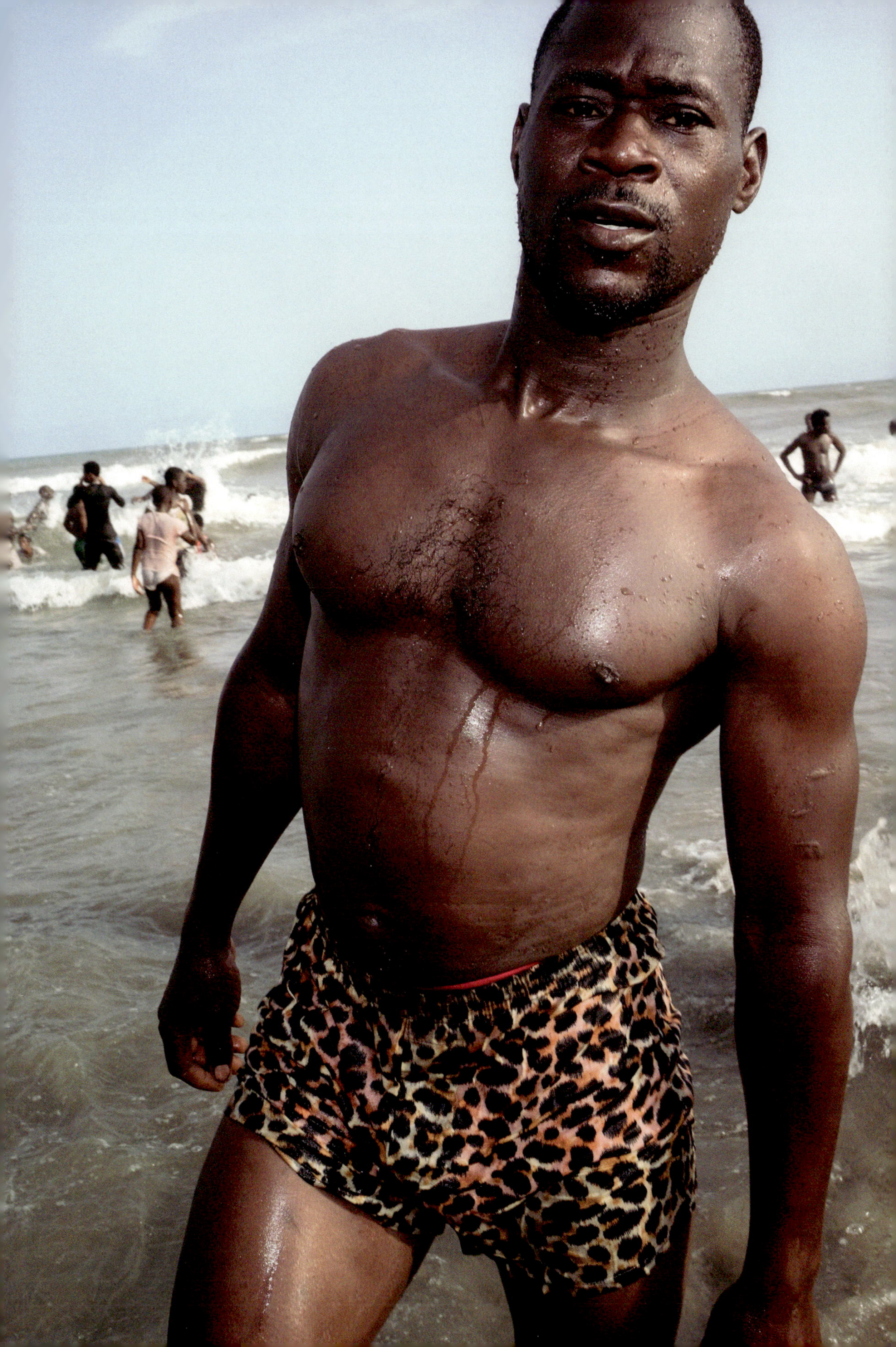

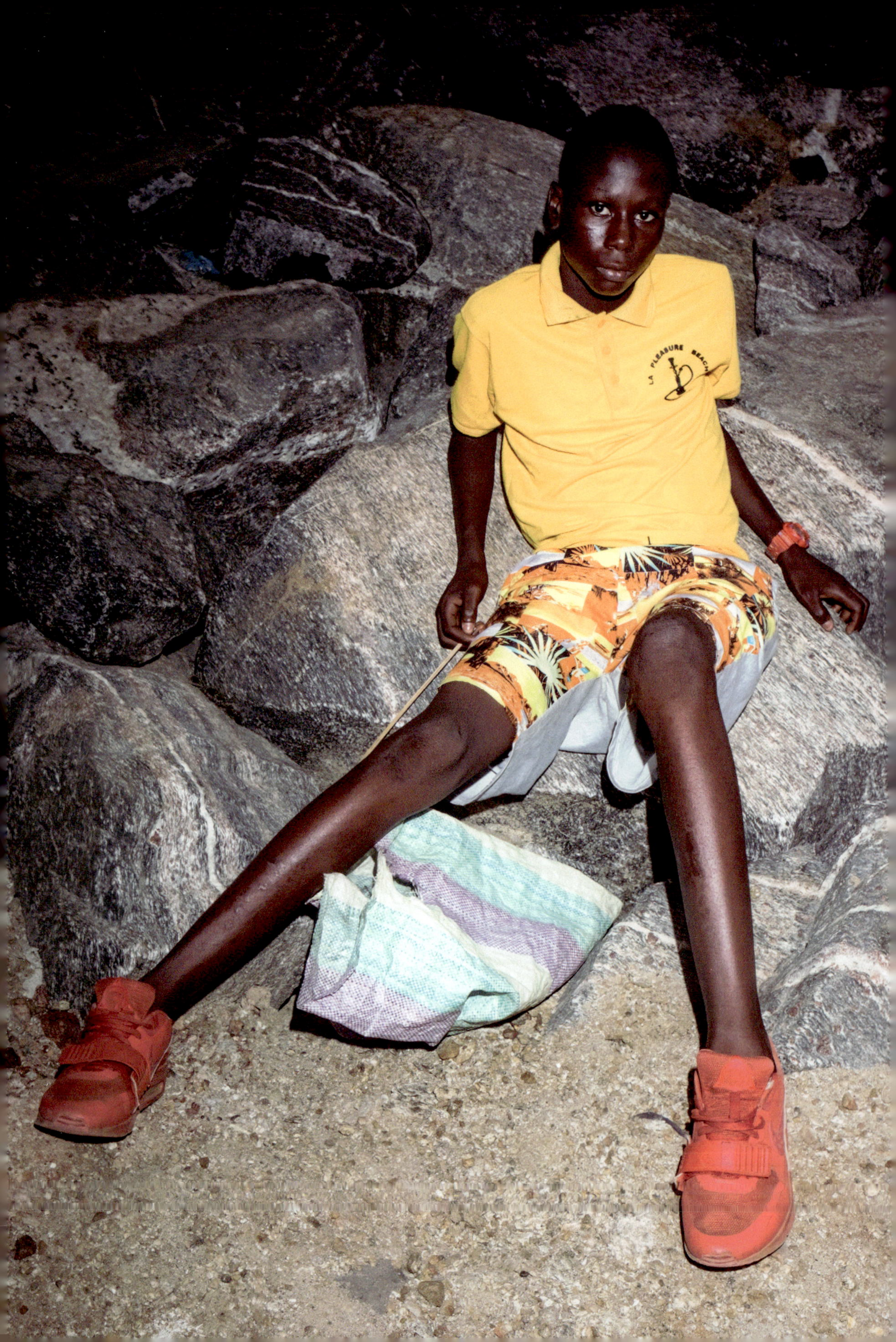
LA PLEASURE BEACH

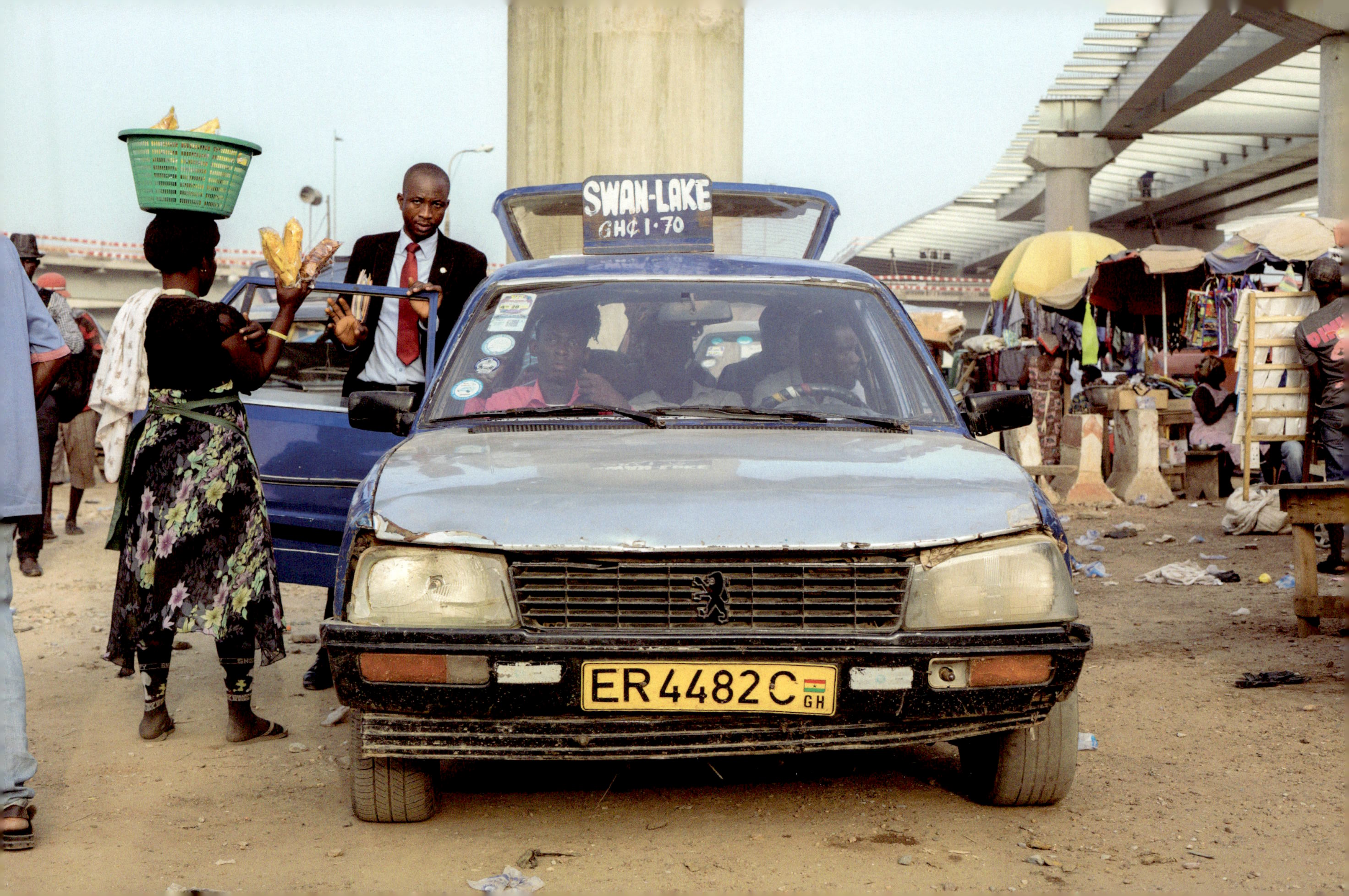

SWAN-LAKE
GH¢ 1·70
ER 4482 C
GH

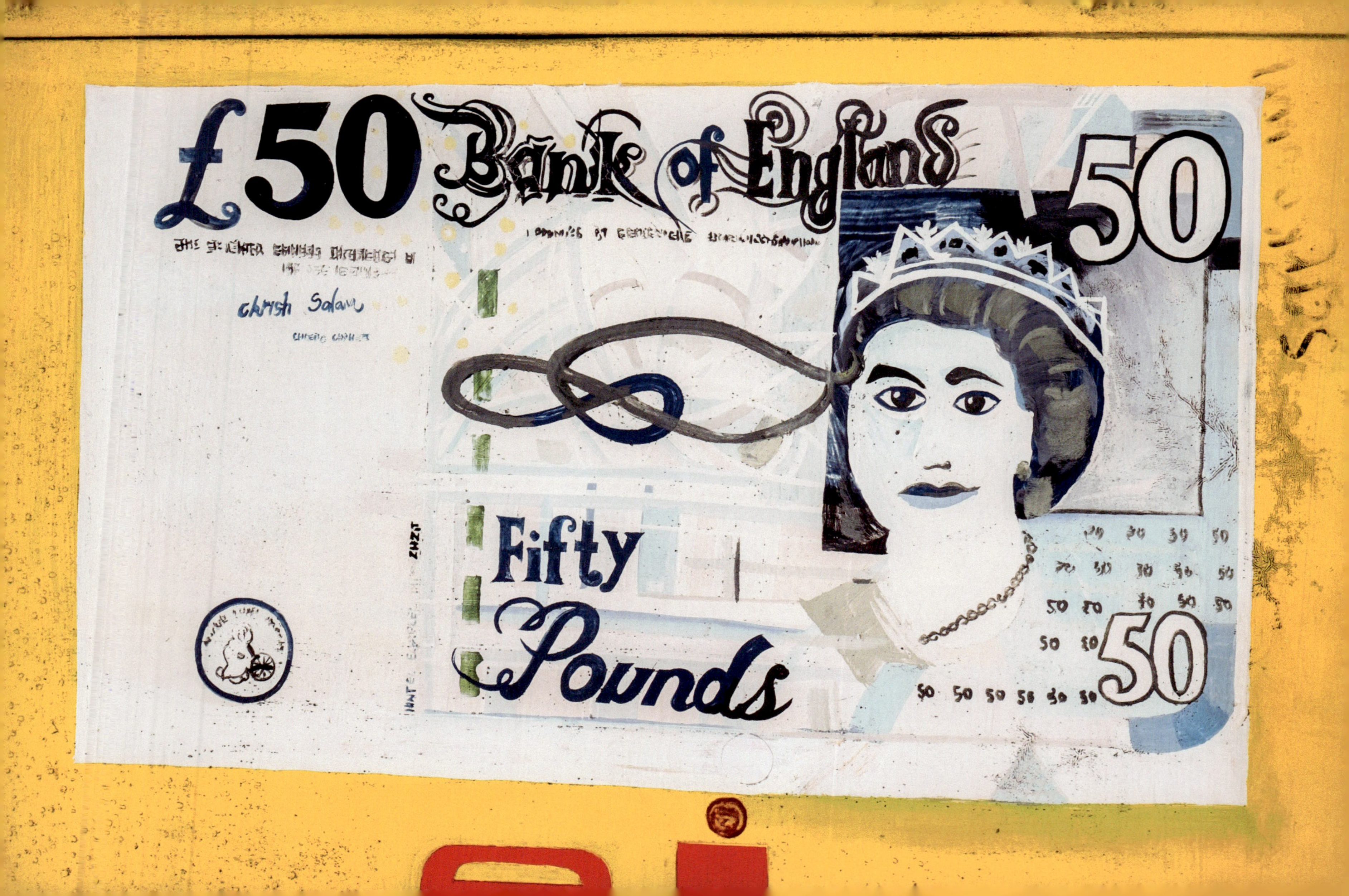

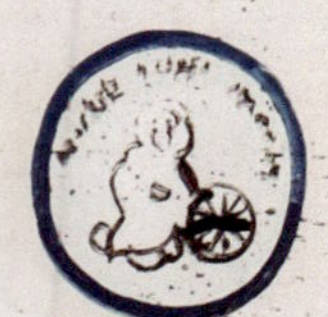

£50
Bank of England
50
chrish Salam
Fifty
Pounds
50

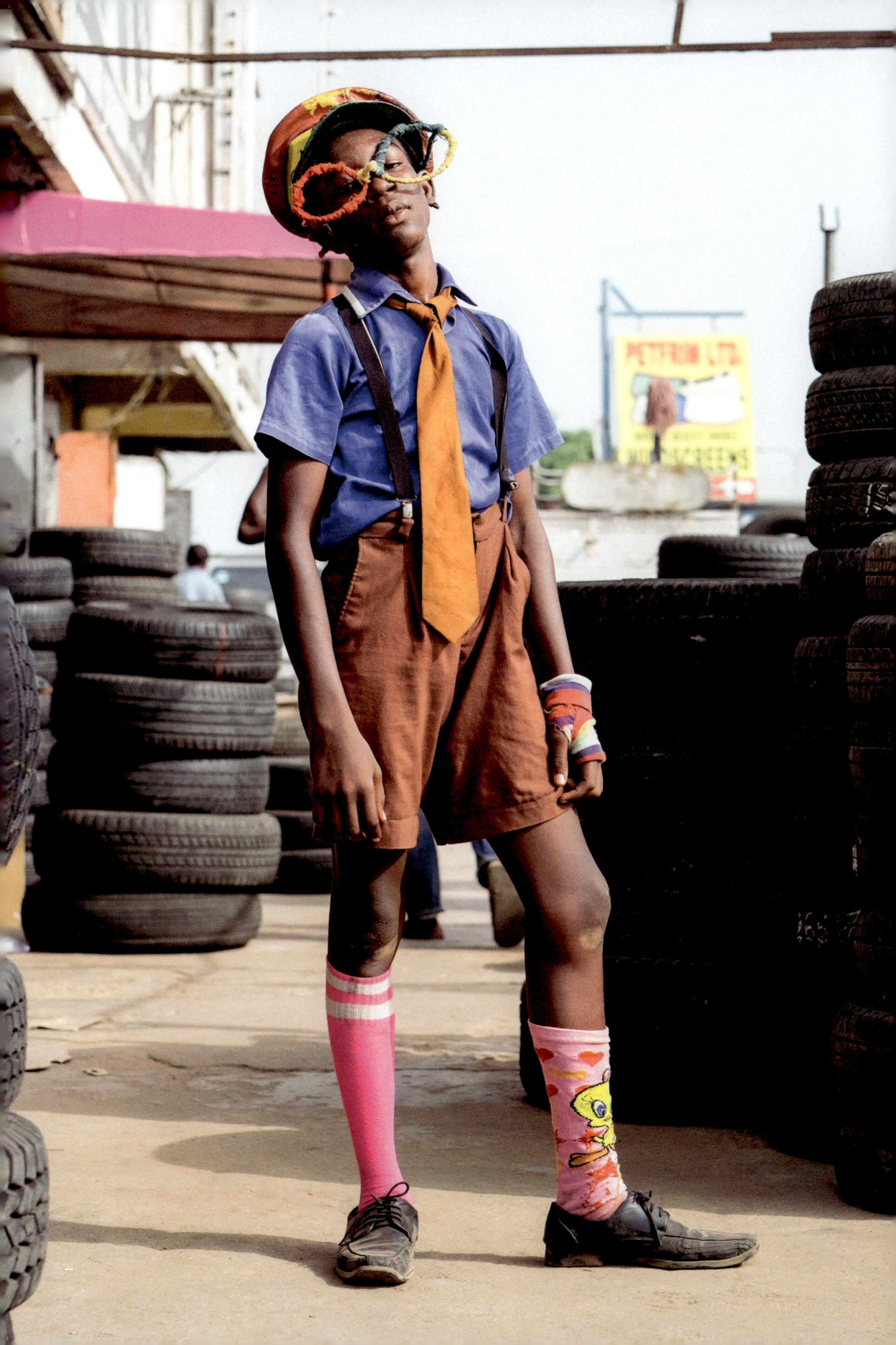

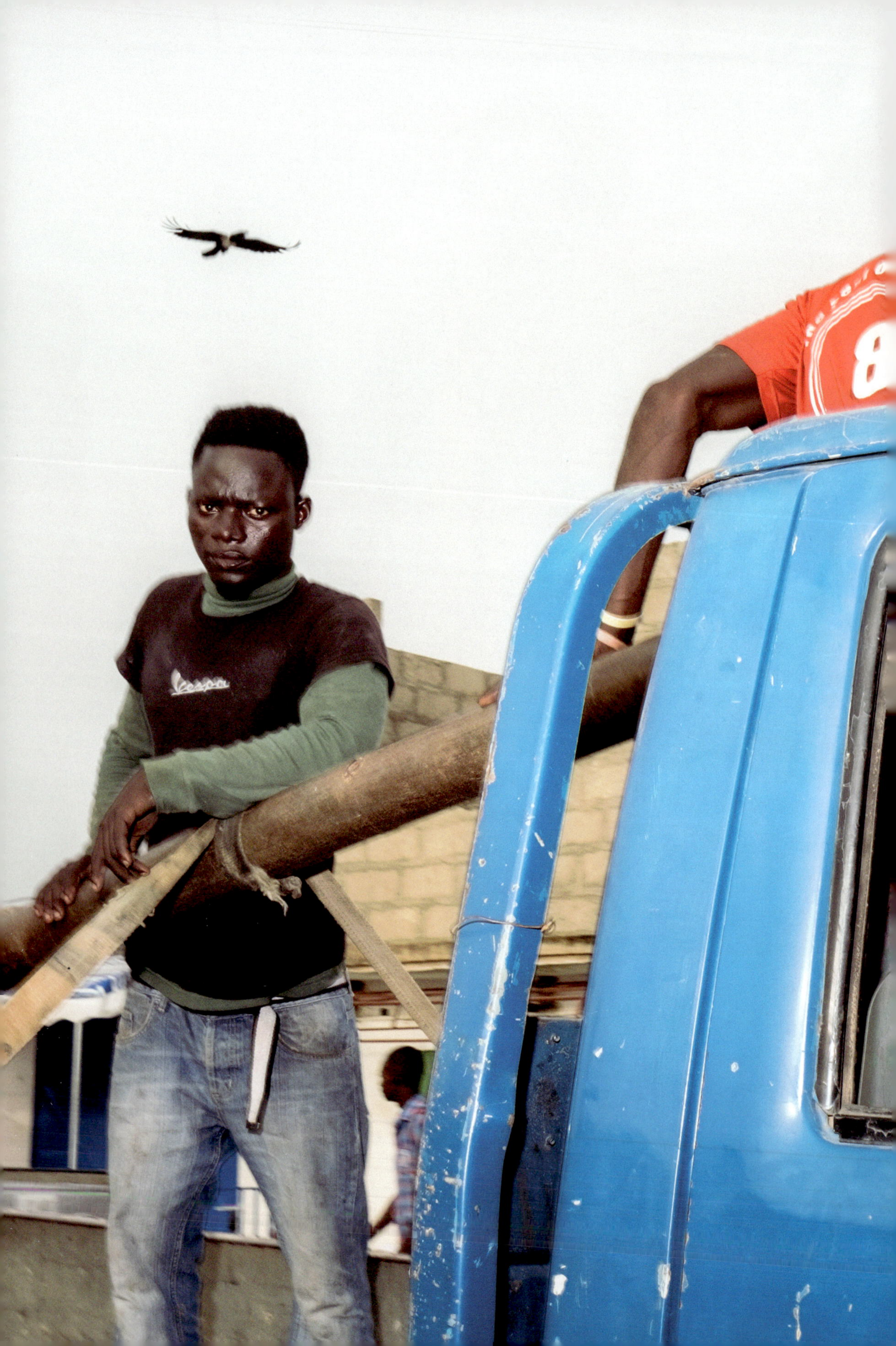
Vespa

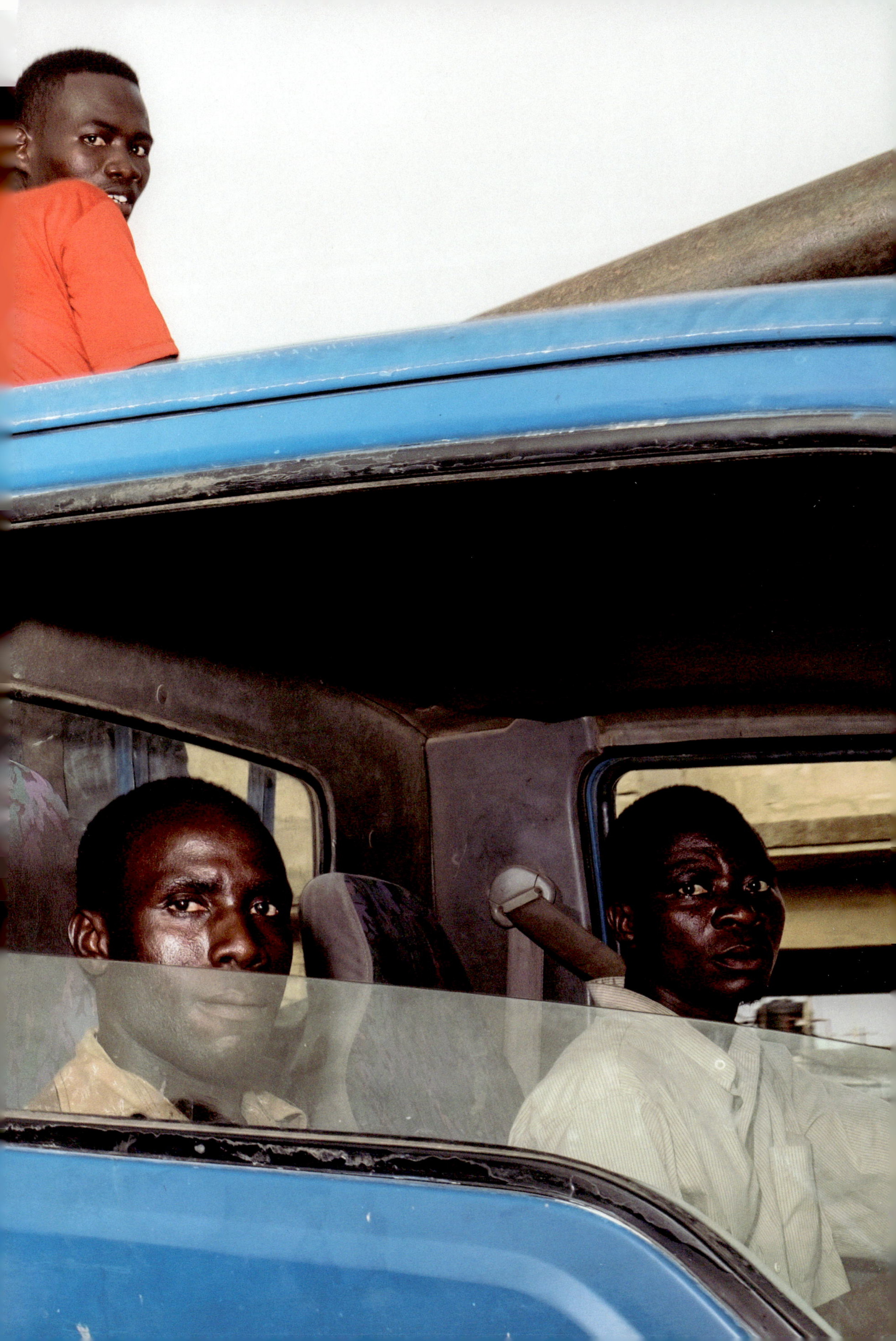

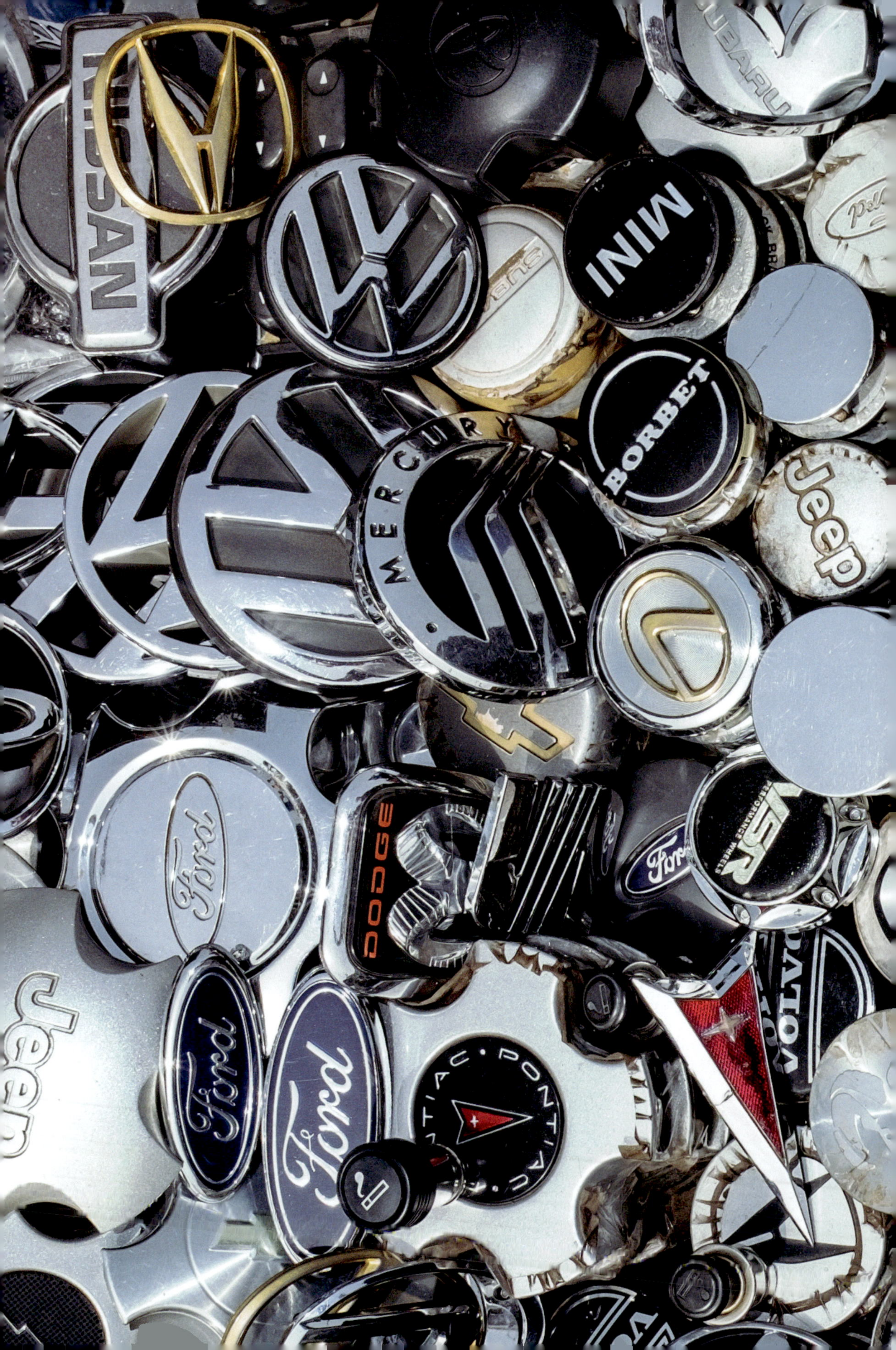
NISSAN
MINI
MERCURY
BORBET
Jeep
Ford
DODGE
Ford
Ford
Jeep
PONTIAC